COPING

<u>W I T H</u>

Money

Richard S. and Mary Price Lee

THE ROSEN PUBLISHING GROUP, INC./NEW YORK

Published in 1988 by The Rosen Publishing Group, Inc.
29 East 21st Street, New York, NY 10010

First Edition

Manufactured in the United States of America

Library of Congress Cataloging-in-Publication Data
Lee, Richard S. (Richard Sandoval), 1927–
    Coping with money.
    Bibliography: p.
    Includes index.
    1. Finance, Personal.   I. Lee, Mary Price.   II. Title.
HG179.L423   1988   332.024   88-18429
ISBN 0-8239-0783-X

For Roger

who has given us years of writing pleasure and
a much valued friendship.

Acknowledgments

Many thanks to our able young typist, Karen Bennis... and to our faithful and good-natured copymachine friend, Carol Gisburne.

We also appreciate the invaluable help of Robert Bazilla, Vice President of the Gallup Organization, in Princeton, New Jersey.

And we thank our young friends Melanie Bryant and Chris and Matt Oberholzer for their input in the form of answers to our informal questionnaire.

Contents

I	Money: Its Importance in Your Life	1
II	Your Parents, Your Money, and You	4
III	Coping with Allowances	11
IV	Designing Your Budget	16
V	Teens Mean Big Dollars for American Business	24
VI	The Basics of Banking and Credit	43
VII	Stocks and Bonds, Or How Your Money Can Make Money—Maybe	53
VIII	How to Earn Money On Your Own	60
IX	Finding a Job Out There	97
X	Operating Your Own Business: Is It for You?	108
XI	Planning for College: A Matter of Mind and Money	115
XII	What's on Your Money–Career Horizon?	125
	Bibliography	131
	Index	132

CHAPTER 1

Money: Its Importance in Your Life

Does this describe you and money?

- I never have enough.
- My parents won't give me my allowance if they're angry with me.
- I can't seem to save money.
- All the things I want are expensive.

Or is this more your experience with money?

- I have always had plenty of money because I have a good job.
- My family talks over my money needs with me and gives me enough to have fun with my friends.

• I have a savings account that is earning money all the time.

Probably you find yourself somewhere between the two extremes. Actually, *no one* has enough money. Keeping dollars in your pocket is a universal problem. Money plays a disappearing act the best magician can't equal.

This book is all about coping with money. The goal is to make money a tool *you* can control, not a problem for you to deal with.

Money is full of contradictions. It is a joy; it is also a responsibility. Money may cause trouble with your family, but dealing with it realistically can also bring a new family closeness. Money can be a false status symbol because it seems to make you popular with your friends. Money, in short, plays a major part in your life.

Coping With Money looks into all these money concerns. Here are some other subjects the book explores:

• Bank accounts.
• Allowances.
• Applying for jobs.
• Saving money for college.
• What jobs parents should pay you for.
• Budgeting for clothes.
• Approaching your parents when you need money.
• Money problems of low-income families.

What you do with your money is of national interest. Each year U.S. teens spend over $30.5 billion of their own money and $40 billion of their parents' money. Teens are often encouraged by their parents to choose household items and to help decide on vacation plans or the purchase of a car.

Since you spend for yourself and your family, it's important to get full value for your dollar. The following chapters will show you how.

CHAPTER 2

Your Parents, Your Money, and You

You may be surprised to learn how great a role your parents play in the important matter of your money.

(We recognize that today a family is not always two parents and their children. A family may be a single parent, a parent and a stepparent—maybe grandparents. This book will use the words "parents," "Mom," and "Dad," realizing, however, that households vary.)

Why should families have trouble dealing with money? Money is, after all, only paper and coins. It is a tool to help provide things that you need. Money is a resource, not a cause for disagreement or worry.

Unfortunately, though, money takes on certain overtones, many of them negative. This is particularly true within the family. Children may place unfair demands on the family for money. There may be constant worrying over how the family paycheck should be spent. Money can be a subtle tool by which a parent can give or deny a young person affection.

Or it can be a great learning experience. Parents can teach their children how to handle money well. The teenager who learns how to get the best for his dollar now will be ready to handle his finances as an adult.

Some parents may not be the best role models when it comes to money. They are not setting a good example if they overuse credit cards, juggle their checkbooks, or are besieged by credit card payments and overdue bills. Consciously or unconsciously, families pass on their habits, so you may find yourself overspending, too.

Today, some families are spending more than ever. Part of this increased spending is due to the sizable income of a two-career family. This comfortable joint income offers pleasures, but problems, too.

The main problem is overemphasis on material things. What were once considered luxuries are now necessities. Families may spend freely to update an already adequate kitchen. Children follow suit by pushing to remodel their bedrooms. They want the best because they see their parents buy the best.

Things, things, things, become the important issue—the latest gadget, whether it costs $10 or $1,000, is a "must." And parents work hard to provide these often unnecessary "musts."

But many parents are concerned about so much affluence. They want their children to have the things their friends have but are also alarmed if they see money spent too freely. Often families live in communities that overemphasize material values. When expensive cars, boats, and motor homes fill driveways and garages, neighboring teens are going to want their own luxuries. Parents have a hard time standing firm when they can't or won't meet these demands. Also, affluence is often temporary. A job layoff or tremendous college costs may require sudden trimming of financial sails. In such cases many of the frills must go.

If your parents are in a high income bracket, you may feel that it's okay for them to pay all your high school expenses, school holiday trips, and other heavy-duty expenses. Actually, they're doing you no favor. They are not teaching you to be self-reliant if they meet all your needs. You won't know how to save or what to buy if others simply hand you life's luxuries. So pitch in financially whether you need to or not.

It may be, on the other hand, that your family has trouble covering expenses. In this situation you as a member of the family may help make decisions about which expenditures are important and which are not.

In either situation you have a vested interest in spending money well. You will also want to have some long-range plans. Your budget (see Chapter 4) should include down-the-road goals as well as things for the present. Perhaps you need to save money for college, or you may simply want to have a substantial amount in your savings account.

Your budget may also include donations to church or synagogue or "adopting" a needy child in a foreign country. In the latter case, you might want to contribute a share of the $20 to $25 a month that your family pays to cover such a youngster's daily needs. Finally, if your family is struggling to make ends meet, you may want to contribute some of your earnings to help out.

As mentioned earlier, money is more than simply purchasing power. Money carries feelings with it and can often be used in a negative way. For instance, parents may unconsciously equate money with love and give their children money as an expression of their love.

Parents often bribe or reward their children with money instead of giving them attention or consideration. Giving money is their way of making up for the things they haven't done for their kids.

They may also withhold money to show disapproval. When parents do this, many teens see it as a lack of love. They also see it as punishment. Money becomes a "negative" when it is used to manage another person.

But mostly, parents try to meet their children's needs for money and take pleasure in watching them spend it well. Parents want to teach their kids that money has to do with responsibility as well as pleasure. With this attitude, money takes its proper place in the family.

One way to develop a positive approach to money is through family meetings. Such powwows give parents and offspring a chance to air their money peeves and make money decisions.

Today's family meetings may have a new dimension. Teenagers of working parents often do much of the purchasing for the household. So meetings are not a formality —the children are part of a working unit.

Get-togethers around the kitchen table also give teens a chance to express their money needs. Young people are constantly short of funds because goods are so expensive today. If this is happening to you, explain to your parents that you feel the same financial pressures that they feel. Just as they have to pay inflated prices for an item such as a dishwasher, you too may not be able to meet skyrocketing prices on a purchase. If you are in a similar bind, perhaps they will understand. You could ask whether they will contribute to your upcoming purchase if you will earn the rest of the money for it.

Family talks serve other purposes. They may reveal how the family stands financially. A family talk can give your parents a chance to express their money concerns. They can avoid all sorts of misunderstandings by letting you in on any financial crisis.

Parents may not want to divulge their salaries, but they can tell you what percentage of their paycheck goes to what part of the family budget. This gives you some insight into how the financial end of the household works. It may also help you understand why parents do not have endless amounts of money to give you. Discussing how money is being spent and actually taking part in some of the decisions will give you experience in handling your own money.

Your parents probably give you a pretty free hand in spending your money, whether allowance money or your own earnings. But some input from them may be helpful. They've learned a few things by making their own mistakes through the years, and those mistakes could be good lessons for you. Many an adult has bought a secondhand car, for instance, and bought someone else's headaches with it. Your parents through their own experiences may be able to help you avoid buying a lemon of a used car.

So parents *can* play on your team. You can enjoy the pleasure of buying things by sharing your interests and opinions. That way money does what it is meant to do— buy you things that you need and that give you pleasure.

How important a role does money play in your life? (That is, do you *have* to have it to be happy?)

Most things I need for "daily existence" are provided, so I only use money for things I want. Money isn't that important, because I have few regular bills. I'm not sad when I don't have money, because I can always play my guitar, piano, or sports, which don't cost anything.

—Matthew Oberholzer

To me, it's not the money itself, it's the things that I can do with it. But money itself doesn't create happiness; if I could do things that didn't require money, I would be happy without it. Unfortunately, mostly everything I do or everywhere I go, money is needed. So I feel it's essential.

—Melanie Bryant

I don't have to be happy and have money at the same time. I can deal with life without money by enjoying things that have no price tag, like friends and family.

—Christopher Oberholzer

Do you have any money problems with your parents? Do they approve of the way you spend it?

A few times during the winter I ask for $5 for gas, but my parents want to reimburse me for gas money I already spent. My parents remind me to take some of the lump sum to the bank, but other than this, they approve.

—Matthew Oberholzer

The only money problem I have with my parents is that I don't get any allowance daily. I usually spend my money on hair products, clothes, jewelry, and other personal products, so I guess they approve. They never really say much about how I spend it unless it's their money.

—Melanie Bryant

Sometimes I am foolish and make unwise decisions and then they get concerned. But most of the time they trust me.

—Christopher Oberholzer

CHAPTER 3

Coping With
Allowances

T he entire question of allowances involves many factors, ranging from practical to philosophical.

On the practical plane, your parents' ability to give you what you consider an adequate allowance depends first of all on their income. Obviously the needs of the family come first, and allowance money may represent an unaffordable frill if the financial situation is tight.

On the philosophical plane, many parents have very definite ideas about the value—even the advisability—of giving money to their children. They believe that they are responsible for guiding and providing for their youngsters and that they know best what the children should have and what is inappropriate.

Most parents, however, do conform to the current trend to give their children a specific amount of money weekly or monthly to spend as they wish.

Allowances usually grow with the teenager. Boys and girls thirteen to fifteen receive around $15 a week. Upper teens (sixteen to nineteen) may get close to $25. But many older teenagers stop receiving allowances because they are earning enough money to support their needs.

Another question that arises with allowances is whether or not a "price tag" is involved. Some parents expect their children to do household chores in exchange for a weekly payment. Others provide the allowance with "no strings attached."

Of course, young people are part of the family and usually are expected to contribute their share to the smooth running of the household. Traditional chores for teens are making their own beds, helping with dishes, and taking out the trash; these tasks have nothing to do with the allowance.

Some parents, on the other hand, expect considerably more work of young people, including baby-sitting, lawn-mowing, and floor-scrubbing. A 1987 Gallup Youth Survey found that teens across the country do rather hefty household and yard work in return for their allowances.

Many parents bypass allowances altogether. They simply hand out money when it is requested. That doesn't mean that they become the Bank of America for their kids—rather, they comply with what they consider reasonable requests. Many teens don't like the uncertainty of this method. "I don't want to beg and pester my parents for money," comments a high school senior. "I want to be able to count on a certain amount each week."

Another teen dislikes what she calls the cross-examination she gets when her family gives her money. "They're always asking me how I spent it. It really makes me feel uncomfortable."

These are among the reasons why handouts generally don't work as well as a weekly (or monthly) allowance. You need to convince your parents that you will spend your allowance wisely but you want to do it your way. Having steady money gives you a feeling of independence.

Of course, that independence may backfire. You're bound to spend some of your money in an unrealistic way. But making mistakes with your allowance is simply a learning process. If you spend too much on something that doesn't work or isn't a quality product, you probably won't make the same mistake again.

What is the definition of a good allowance? A good allowance should serve your needs and wants. Needs may include school expenses such as bus fare and lunches, church contributions, haircuts, and basic grooming items. The "wants" are more fun. They include snacks, magazines, tapes, hobbies, school dances, and perhaps saving for an expensive item like a camera.

Some of the "wants" may cost more than you have. To bridge the difference you may have to supplement your allowance with a job.

How often should allowances be given? While early teens may receive an allowance every week, those about to graduate from high school may be given money on a quarterly basis. If you are an older teen, you may like the quarterly setup. For instance, if your allowance is $180 quarterly, you can calculate how to make it last. This "dividing the pie" is good practice for the future, too.

Not all parents believe in allowances. Phyllis Diller, the comedian, is one of them. "I really feel that giving a teenager an allowance is like feeding a lion a pound of raw hamburger and telling him he's going to get it only once a week. He'll eat you alive. Bah! Humbug! Let them work. It's the only way they'll learn about life." There's no doubt where Miss Diller stands on money and teens!

WHO RECEIVES ALLOWANCES?

	Yes	No	Average weekly allowance
NATIONAL	46%	54%	$10.00
Male	47	53	$ 8.39
Female	45	55	$11.71
Ages 13 to 15	55	45	$ 8.46
Ages 16 to 17	33	67	$13.74
White-collar family background	46	54	$ 9.81
Blue-collar family background	48	52	$10.36
East	45	55	$ 8.60
Midwest	48	52	$11.34
South	51	49	$ 9.51
West	38	62	$10.75
Central cities	53	47	$13.95
Suburbs	47	53	$ 9.04
Nonmetropolitan areas	42	48	$ 8.47

Source: Gallup Youth Survey, 1987.

Approximately how much spending money do you have per week?

I take spending money out of a lump sum that accumulates over two-three weeks of work. I usually put everything above $50 into the bank, and I rarely spend all of the $50. (It carries over to the next accumulation.)

—Matthew Oberholzer

I have at least $5 a week. I rarely have more unless it's for a specific thing, not just to spend.

—Melanie Bryant

I have about $5 to $10 a week to spend.

—Christopher Oberholzer

CHAPTER 4

Designing Your Budget

I f Phyllis Diller thinks allowances are a rip-off, maybe she'd be kinder about budgets. Teens who can budget their money will always find it easier to have what they want because they've planned ahead and saved.

For many teens, an allowance and an outside income make it fairly simple to plan a comfortable budget. The hard part may be allocating a part of that budget for savings. Saving is hardly Fun City because there are always things you'd like to do with your money right now! But if you learn to put some money "on hold" (10 percent is a workable amount, at least to start with), you'll do yourself two favors. One, you will have the money when you need it most; and two, you'll be forming good habits for lifetime saving. So when you design your budget, be sure there is a place for savings in it.

Although it's not necessary, you'll probably have better success with savings if you have a goal in mind: your own car, a special trip, a CD player; or that really big show, college. Saving is much more interesting if you set your sights on something, then predict when you'll be able to have it based on the regular amounts you save.

When you save for a major item, you actually save twice, and perhaps even three times. First, your savings earn money in a bank account. Second, since you'll have the money for what you want, you'll save the cost of interest on a loan. Finally, you may save even more money by paying cash.

As you'll see in Chapter 11, going to college is extremely expensive. If you make a college budget for the total cost or just for your incidentals, you may want to make a separate savings category for these special expenses. That way, you could save X dollars a month for college and Y dollars a month for a boom box or whatever else you have in mind.

Other elements of your budget would include the fixed expenses we've mentioned such as transportation, school lunches, and supplies, and the "pleasure expenses," the ongoing costs of hobbies, collecting, tapes, movies, small trips, and perhaps clothes. Balancing these expenses would be your allowance, gifts of money, and whatever you can earn from a regular part-time job or in bits and pieces.

In short form, a budget framework could look like this. Many variations are possible; you can create and follow the budget plan that suits you best:

FIXED EXPENSES	
Transportation	
Lunches	
School supplies	
Other (clothes, etc.)	
	Total _____
DISCRETIONARY EXPENSES	
Entertainment and dating	
Refreshments	

	Total _____
Hobbies	
Books, records, tapes	
Other (gasoline, etc.)	
SAVINGS	
Gifts (holiday, birthday, etc.)	
Special funds (car, investments, major purchase)	
Travel	
College	
INCOME OTHER THAN ALLOWANCE	
Gifts	
Earnings	
Miscellaneous	
TOTAL WEEKLY/MONTHLY EXPENSES	
TOTAL OTHER INCOME	
WEEKLY/MONTHLY ALLOWANCE	

SAVINGS — Total _____

INCOME OTHER THAN ALLOWANCE — Total other income _____

A teenager in Washington, D.C. keeps a balanced budget much like this one, but her clothing needs are handled differently. Her parents give her a predetermined amount twice a year for clothes. This is a sensible way to handle this expense because—let's face it!—teen clothes are a big item in any budget. This teen can make major purchases based on her allotment. When she has spent her half-yearly amount, she knows she'll have a dry spell until the next payment. Teens who budget for clothes on their own should plan on setting aside about 15 percent of total income for this purpose.

Clothing is one big item no matter how you budget for it, and dating is another. (Yes, the word "dating" has come back into the language, rejoining the phrase "get together.") But whether it's a date or getting together, the costs of a day or evening of fun can give even the best-run budget a rough time. (For the item that really can dent a budget, see Chapter 5 about the senior prom!)

Unfortunately, the old dating rules don't apply the way they used to, and this can cause problems. Until recently, dating always meant the boy paid. But today girls often share the costs for a movie or a fast-food snack. Some girls are happy to chip in because they like the feeling of independence that comes with paying one's own way. And because many older girls work as hard and earn as much as boys, they have the money to spend. Finally, everything is so expensive today that many boys cannot afford to take girls out without some financial help.

But sharing the date costs brings with it some problems that don't relate to money itself. Teens of both sexes are not quite sure when they should pay, when they should go halves, and exactly what sharing the check means.

First, let's look at what some girls are asking themselves: "If I offer to pay, will he think I'm really saying he's too poor to take me out?" Or, "If I don't offer to pay, do I lose my independence and my right to say no to a good-night kiss?"

Boys are just as confused. Many are embarrassed to let a girl pay her way. Others feel that girls who split the bill—independent girls—still expect to have doors opened for them and other traditional date courtesies. What's a guy to do?

Then there's the possibility of a girl asking a boy for a date, even a first date. Fine, say some boys when asked about this tables-turned etiquette. But then the girl may expect the boy to pay for the date. Not so fine! If girls do the asking, shouldn't they do the paying? Again, confusing questions surround an old custom, the date.

Of course, many girls would never consider paying for a date. Their reasons are many, tradition being the main one. But another factor of this no-sharing attitude is that girls sometimes equate money with love. The more a boy spends on them, the more proof it is of his interest and affection.

Leslie Jane Nonkin, author of *I Wish My Parents Understood Me, A Report on the Teenage Female*, asked over one thousand girls how they felt about paying for dates. Forty percent of those surveyed felt that a date was the boy's responsibility. Another 14 percent were undecided. But 55 percent of the girls who did the asking still felt the boy should pick up the tab.

Obviously, the votes are not in on who pays the check. Maybe that's just as well. This way, you can negotiate a date as it comes along and do what feels most comfortable. Also, the better you know your date, the more up-front both of you can be about deciding who pays for what. Many smart teens of both sexes solve all (or most) of the uncertainty by splitting the costs of an outing, or one pays for the movies while the other springs for the burgers and fries.

Dates may be negotiable, but there's one other money area—a big one—where you may have to go it alone: automobile insurance. Driving is very expensive, even if you don't own a car. The insurance premiums your parents pay for their car will go up sharply when your name is added to the policy. (If you have driver training in school before you get your license, the premium may not go up quite as much. Be sure to mention this to the insurance company when your name is added to the policy.) Many young people take over this added money responsibility as a fair exchange for the privilege of driving the family car.

The increase in the insurance premium may not seem fair to you, but insurance companies have found that on the average teen drivers are not good insurance risks. Their rates remain higher until they're over twenty-one (up to twenty-five for men in many cases).

There's a kind of reverse incentive for driving safely. If you have no tickets for moving violations and no accidents for three years, the premiums may go down somewhat. But if you do have a reported traffic offense or an accident, those high costs will, alas, usually go even higher—sometimes even if an accident is not your fault.

As with a major purchase, you can save toward your insurance by putting away 1/52nd of your share of the premiums every week, or, if you're managing a monthly budget, 1/12th every month. Then, when your parents get their yearly or six-month insurance bill, you'll have the money to pay your share. A tip: Put away a little more than what you need for insurance. Premiums are constantly rising and this way you'll be covered. If in six months or a year your family's rate has not gone up beyond the added premium for you, you'll have some "found" money.

There are several ways to compartmentalize a budget so it does everything you hope it will. One way is to put everything into one savings account except what you need for fixed expenses and weekend recreation. Then keep a notebook in which you reserve specific amounts in your account for different items.

If you find this doesn't work because you "borrow" money you're saving for one thing to buy another, you may want to use your savings account only for long-term goals, and steel yourself not to make withdrawals from it. You could even have two accounts, or a combination of accounts and piggy banks, lock boxes, even envelopes. It doesn't matter how you run your budget as long as you set your goals, then do your very best to stick to them. Nowhere is it written that this will be easy!

A budget can do something else you might not expect:

show you how possible (or impossible) certain things can be. Knowing this helps you establish your priorities and decide what things are really worth saving for and what you can live without.

Let's say you, like one young lady, decide you *must* have a horse. Can you? Designing a budget can answer the question, especially when your parents can't contribute to your project. When you figure the purchase price, it may seem do-able. But when you add the cost of stabling, feed, tack, shoeing, and the inevitable veterinary bills, you may find as she did that you would have to give up too many other things to make the horse affordable.

Your budget will bring you face to face with reality, it's true. But good things can happen if you stick to it. Such as maybe a little money to spare!

Do you budget any of your money—plan ahead how you're going to spend, or save it?

As I've written, I keep $50 out of the bank to spend. This limits me from buying anything more than that amount. In the back of my mind, though, $20 is set aside for "nights on the town." I keep $30 for anything I see that I might want to buy (clothes, sheet music, etc.).

—Matthew Oberholzer

Sometimes when I'm out window-shopping, I'll see something that I want badly and when I get my money I save it. (As long as the item isn't over $40 because I'll end up spending some of the money.) But I don't really ever have enough money to budget it out. I just buy what's needed at the time that I receive the money.

—Melanie Bryant

Sometimes I deposit an amount of money in the bank. Usually I like to have money around, in case I need it.

—Christopher Oberholzer

CHAPTER 5

Teens Mean Big Dollars for American Business

A national survey shows that teenagers not only spend large amounts of their own money but also help decide how their parents' money is spent. More than half of the $70.5 billion you spent in a recent year belonged to your parents. This participation makes you young people a very powerful segment of the consumer population.

That doesn't mean that you helped yourself to the family savings. Your parents may have encouraged you to choose the cereals, magazines, and other household goods you felt the family would enjoy. You may even have been asked what car the family should buy, and where to go on vacations.

Parents are inviting you to make such decisions because of your knowledge of consumer goods. Television advertising is one reason you know about today's products. The commercials may color your interests, and you in turn pass this enthusiasm on to your parents. Yours is the first generation to influence purchases so strongly.

DO THE FAMILY GROCERY SHOPPING

	Most of the time	Occasionally	Rarely	Never
NATIONAL	8%	26%	35%	31%
Male	5	24	38	33
Female	11	29	31	29
Ages 13 to 15	8	24	36	32
Ages 16 to 18	9	29	33	29
Whites	8	25	36	31
Blacks	19	23	26	32
White-collar family background	6	33	34	27
Blue-collar family background	11	22	33	34
East	7	25	33	35
Midwest	6	27	37	30
South	13	29	29	29
West	8	23	41	28
Central cities	8	29	30	33
Suburbs	7	25	39	29
Nonmetropolitan areas	11	27	31	31

Source: Gallup Youth Survey, 1987.

Why do you buy and *how* do you buy? The answers to these questions may surprise you. On the surface, a person appears to buy something simply because he or she needs that item. But there are many unconscious reasons for plunking down small and large sums of money for new things. For instance, did you ever notice that your spirits go up after a shopping spree? That's because buying things makes you feel independent, makes you feel good, lets you bask in your friends' approval.

Advertisers try to promote those feelings. They imply that you won't be quite as worthwhile without their product. You may take this hard sell seriously and put pressure on your parents. If they have money problems, that puts them in a difficult position. They may have to refuse you, and you take the refusal the wrong way. You may feel they don't care enough about you to put up the cash for a "vital" purchase. But if you think a moment, you'll realize that you don't need material goods from your family to know that they care about you.

As teens, your spending patterns are very different from those of other age groups. Friends can play a major role in the unique ways you use your money. With a little persuasion from them, you may decide to blow your entire savings on something you "cannot do without." Peer pressure to spend freely is increasing. The whole problem of cash access can be shattering when you can't keep up with your friends.

Susan Johns of Denver, Colorado, wanted desperately to go on a white-water canoeing trip with her friends, but the family business was in such bad shape that there were no extra dollars for this expensive spree. John Howard of Los Angeles, California, reports that he was on the phone talking to a friend who had just bought a new sports car when he looked out the window to see *his* family's car being repossessed.

A recent issue of *Seventeen* told these unhappy stories and more as the magazine considered the question of what teens should do when they can't keep up with their friends' spending. According to the article, many young people hang around with groups of wealthy friends and feel very empty inside. "I'm really different," one laments, "because they accept me as someone who *seems* like them but really is *not*. They have endless money, and I can barely scrape enough together to rent a tape."

Some teens manage not to let spending—or lack of it— become a major issue. They do this by realizing that their friends like them for what they are, not what they have. They feel good enough about themselves not to be super-envious of the big spenders.

Other teens find out that extra money does not always make them as deliriously happy as they thought they would be. The *Seventeen* article noted that a teen in Syracuse, New York, worked all year to save enough money for a prom dress. When the prom was over, she found that life was not that much more terrific. The prom had been fun but she was still the same person—liked by some, not liked by others. The moral? Having money is nice, but it won't radically alter the problems and challenges that you have to meet in life.

Speaking of proms and prom dresses, they *do* cost money. Several hundred dollars may have slipped through your fingers before you take those first steps on the dance floor.

What are some of the things that make a prom so expensive? For one thing, high school proms in the school gymnasium—cost-free—became less popular. At some schools this biggest dance of the year may now be held at a fine hotel. (However, prohibitive outside costs have recently brought the decorated gym back on the scene again.) Second, the family car won't do anymore. Something flashier is in order. The Philadelphia *Inquirer* comments that many young suburbanites go to the prom by limousine. (Three couples may chip in for one limo to keep the price down.)

Do teenagers mind putting out a small fortune for one evening's entertainment? Not Paul Langlois from Henderson High School in West Chester, Pennsylvania. "I saved the money I made from last summer just for our prom. Now it's all gone, but it was worth it."

The prom is a one-time expense. What are some of the other things teens do with their money? One fact stands out clearly. You buy independently of your parents. Actually, you may go out of your way to buy things that totally contradict your parents' tastes and wishes. After all, no teen wants to be found agreeing with his parents!

On the other hand, your parents have been at this buying business longer than you, and they naturally want you to benefit from their experience. And let's face it—parents can influence your shopping because they supply your money. If your allowance and job income are small, you may look to them for help. Whether you get it or not depends on your relationship with them (and their financial resources).

Parents tend to give in to pleas for money because of today's more permissive climate. Also, parents are generally no match for television's hard sell. A recent survey showed that by the time children graduate from high school they have soaked up 15,000 hours of television and have watched nearly 64,000 commercials. Many of those ads lean on parents to open their wallets to their children. And many parents do.

You teens are a major audience for television commercials. Everything you have ever dreamed of greets you in larger-than-life living color. Commercials promise instant beauty, popularity, and excitement if you purchase their products. We would all like to have these attractive assets, but we don't necessarily get them from owning a particular car or buying a certain lip gloss.

A recent TV ad showed a handsome young man trying out his new car. His friends watched in admiration as he drove the car at breakneck speed. The subtle message of the pitch was that you, too, will suddenly be the center of attention if you choose this car.

Advertisements in magazines like *Teen* and *Seventeen* show a "10" girl wearing a popular lip gloss. In the background two guys look longingly at her. The message? The lip gloss will change your life. In fact, while it may help you look attractive, it doesn't guarantee that the boys will come running.

A recent ad in a teen magazine offered a kit from a young Hollywood superstar containing a secret love message "just for *you*." Over 50,000 teens responded to the tempting offer!

Television and magazine ads may hook you by asking you to join exciting mail-order record or tape clubs. So far so good. But when you wish to end your membership, you often find the club unwilling to accommodate you. Even though you have bought the number of tapes specified in your agreement, you may find tapes arriving automatically for months to come—along with bills. To prevent this, you have to write "no thanks" (at your expense) each month before the deadline. (The easier way is to return the item unopened to the post office.)

Beware also of:

- Items that are priced to seem less expensive. A four-dollar item seems cheaper when tagged $3.98.

- "Slashed" items, *i.e.*, things that have been re- duced. They may not have been worth more in the first place.
- Exaggeration. "This tissue is so soft on my sore nose that it doesn't even hurt to blow." *No* tissue is that magical for a raw, red nose.

It all comes down to *Caveat emptor*, "Let the buyer beware." This phrase was originated by the Romans, who didn't want to be taken in by false claims. And that was over two thousand years ago!

Merchandisers will still encourage you, however, to shell out your dollars. Teenagers are now such a hot com- modity that entire department stores are being designed to serve your age group. What exactly do these stores stock for your special interests? Clothes, bikes, stereo equip- ment, and fast-food items are among the many products on your shopping lists and in their inventory. And what tops all other types of teenage sales at the moment? Videotape rentals. They seem to take a lot of your money. ("Your money," incidentally, is usually a comfortable $30 a week to spend as you wish.) Records and tapes are also popular items. The average American teenager spends close to $200 a year on these items. No wonder the recording in- dustry looks on your age group as a gold mine.

Although retailers regard teenagers as excellent sources of revenue, teens in turn do not always feel that they are properly treated by store personnel. Shop owners, sales- people, and security guards in department stores and malls sometimes hassle young people because they shop in "packs." The owners worry about their merchandise and the effect that a group of young people may have on other customers. Yet these young people contribute a large part of their profit.

WHERE TEENS SHOP

	Shopping Mall	Downtown stores	Department store
NATIONAL	72%	20%	6%
Male	67	22	7
Female	76	16	5
Ages 13 to 15	75	17	6
Ages 16 to 18	68	22	6
East	71	21	5
Midwest	72	21	4
South	72	19	8
West	72	16	7
Central cities	76	12	11
Suburbs	76	17	5
Nonmetropolitan areas	61	31	4

Source: Gallup Youth Survey, 1987.

Common complaints from mall owners include teens running up and down escalators or stairways and remaining too long in fast-food places. "They watch us like hawks; they won't let us sit on their benches, and they tell us to leave their store if we're not buying anything," one teenager complains. It's true—this loitering annoys shopkeepers. One owner remembers a group of girls spending an hour trying different nail polishes and then walking out of the store without a purchase. To this criticism one teen admitted, "Maybe we do get on their nerves, but we'll probably buy the next time."

Another young shopper comments: "They make us feel like shoplifters. The security guards are always watching us."

They have other complaints. Some center around the merchandise itself. The "in" items seem to be over-priced—"partly, I think," says one shopper, "because they know we will pay any price for something we really want."

So there's basis for complaint on both sides. The best thing to do is to plan your shopping trip with clearcut goals in mind. That eliminates aimless wandering and random handling of merchandise. But merchandisers may not realize just how savvy teenagers are. They shop for quality while seeking a bargain at the same time. "We kids shop so much," comments one teen, "that we know what's going on."

Teens do know what is going on, but there is more to learn on the subject. There is a right and wrong way to go about spending your money, and the previous comments on smart shopping simply skim the surface. More specifically:

- Choose every item with care.
- Buy quality bargains (marked-down name brands with a good reputation).
- Don't over-buy (if you can barely squeeze your clothes into a closet now, why crowd it further?).
- Save your money so that you will have cash for large purchases.

The flip side of spending money wisely is, of course, dribbling it away until you're left with an empty wallet. The answers to the following questions can reveal some bad shopping habits:

- Do you buy without planning ahead?
- Do you buy something at the store nearest you rather than comparison shopping?
- Do you spend money because it "feels good"?

If you have "yeses" for these questions, turn them into "nos" by taping the questions to your dresser mirror. Check at the end of each day to see how many "nos" you scored.

Unwise spending habits are one way to keep you cash-poor. You can also lose out if you're not an experienced shopper. Many things can be done to save money if you know a few consumer basics.

One of them is comparison shopping. Although it may be boring to compare prices on an item, there's nothing boring about saving money. You can save money on everything from cameras and ski equipment to cereals and motor oil when you comparison shop.

A tip when shopping in the supermarket: Choose the store's "house" brand or a generic-labeled item. The price is lower because no fancy packaging or heavy advertising goes into these products.

Believe it or not, you can do much of your comparison shopping in a library. Consumer magazines, particularly *Consumer Reports*, will guide you on the expensive items you plan to buy. These magazines report on the quality of a product and rate it against others of its kind in performance, desirable features, and price.

In a recent *Consumer Reports* guidebook, four pages were devoted to all-terrain bikes. The testers were mainly looking for ease of pedaling in their analyses. At the end of the report were ratings for all the bikes tested. The Bridgestone MB-2 came out on top. At about $400 and thirty-five pounds, it has eighteen speeds and a twenty-six-to-eight gear range. Frame rigidity, pedal quality, and seat comfort were rated excellent. In contrast, the Huffy Scout at $120 (thirty-nine pounds, ten speeds) rated very poorly.

While such magazines can help you decide how to spend

your money, only budgeting will provide that money. Budgeting has already been discussed, but it's worth a brief further mention here.

If you place your job or allowance money in different categories (a budgeted amount for clothes, for recreation, etc.), you will have control over your money. Of course, you have to stick to your spending plan. You can't borrow from one area to fund another. If you have used up the "clothes" portion of your budget but are tempted by a terrific jeans sale, avoid taking money from your "entertainment" pot. Reason? You may suddenly want to do something recreational like going to the movies, but there's no money because you've blown it on new jeans.

Shopping for bargains rounds out the ways that you can save money. Look for discount stores with quality brand names and store-wide and post-season sales. "Irregulars" are also often great clothing bargains. Look at each item carefully for flaws in stitching or weaving; if you can't find them, chances are others won't notice them either.

Some specific items need even closer scrutiny—cosmetics, for instance. A recent survey found that over 68 percent of teenage girls use a makeup base of some sort. To the cosmetics industry, that means well over $450 million a year in their cash registers.

Beauty products that are quite different in price may vary little in content. You may pay $7.95 for a moisturizing cream that contains basically the same ingredients as one selling for $4.95. You probably chose the more expensive cream because it was extensively advertised.

According to the Gallup Youth Survey, two out of three teens buy their own clothes. Traditionally boys are less intense about clothing than girls, but they do have definite preferences. They like to wear things that are accepted by their crowd, but they take less time and spend less money to achieve the same goal. The "right" sweater, shirt, and pants make them comfortable. However, the current trend is for teen boys to wear the latest "look." That means they are putting more money into clothes than ever before.

Teenage girls make clothes the centerpiece of their lives. They want only the latest, most fashionable clothing. Fortunately, they can have it at reasonable prices. Discount stores have copied the fashions shown in expensive clothing shops, and many lower-priced chain stores have their own designer or famous-personality clothing.

Mail-order catalogs also offer clothes that often undersell similar goods in retail stores. This is because catalog printing and mailing costs are considerably less than the overhead for retail stores.

A source of really inexpensive clothes is the secondhand clothing store. In many areas these thrift stores no longer simply offer hand-me-downs. Their recycled clothing is colorful, clean, fashionable—and cheap. Plus the jeans supply is endless.

Another way to save money is to make your own clothes. Put that sewing machine to work and create a blouse or skirt at half or a third the price of a store-bought garment.

Finally, if you are small for your age, you may be able to buy some of your clothes in the girls' or boys' department. A ski jacket in a girls' size 'L' may cost far less than its duplicate in the junior or misses' department. A boy's size 18 jacket could replace a man's size 36 for a lot less money.

Bikes are another major purchase for teens. Here are some hints that will guide you in buying, using, and protecting your bike:

- Shop in bicycle specialty shops that provide parts and service (especially if your bike represents a major investment on your part).

- Test-ride a bike before you decide to buy it.
- Check the frame joints. You want a bike with reinforced joints.
- Have the dealer check wheels and frame for proper adjustment (this should have been done with an expensive, already-assembled bike).
- Better bikes have slip-resistant pedals; look for this feature.
- Buy the finest possible lock to protect your investment—and when you secure your bike, always lock it in as conspicuous a place as possible. (Don't forget to remove the front wheel and secure it with the rest of the bike.)

Skateboards are another form of transportation and recreation. This $300-million-a-year industry caters totally to young people. Just as with bicycles, the more expensive skateboards are safer and more durable. Although you may not want to compete against Tony Hawk of California—Tony can complete two midair somersaults on his wheeled board—you do want a reliable skateboard for zooming along with friends.

If you are sixteen—or have reached the minimum age for your state—you are probably working on a driver's license. Once you have received it, the family car suddenly becomes an object of great interest. If you're allowed to drive your parents' car, you may earn extra driving privileges by checking the oil and tires without being asked, by gassing up for your share of miles (and maybe a little more), and—if you can afford it—by contributing to the extra insurance they'll have to pay because you're driving the car. (How to budget for this expense is covered in Chapter 4.)

Many of you will be looking for a used car. Beware! A

lemon can cost you all your hard-earned cash and then some. Rust spots, squishy shock absorbers, a worn-out engine—these and many other things can have you pouring money into a car as fast as the antifreeze dribbles out of a leaky radiator.

Here are some car-buying tips:

- Do spend a few dollars for a paperback used-car price guide. (Some of these also tell in general terms the strong and weak points of the used cars they cover—valuable information to have.)
- If you are lucky enough to be buying a newer car, try to buy it from a new-car dealer, who is more likely to have reconditioned it in his own shop.
- Do get a car with a warranty if you can afford it (but remember that most older cars, privately sold cars, and high-mileage cars will only be sold as-is).
- Remember that the price of any used car is based on a combination of its original cost, its age, and its mileage. An older car with low mileage is usually the best value for the money you spend—especially if it's one you know about (from a relative or a neighbor).
- Keep in mind that any car that looks as though it has lived an exciting life (a muscle-car or sports car) probably has its best days behind it.
- When you've boiled down your search to one or two likely cars, take along someone who knows cars —perhaps your parents' mechanic—to check out your would-be wheels. Agree on a fee for the mechanic's time.
- Put aside a cash reserve equal to at least 25 percent of what you pay for the car for unexpected repairs. If

you need the money, it's there; if not, it's a good
beginning for your next car if it's kept in a savings
account.
• When you buy, read carefully anything you are asked
to sign so that there are no misunderstandings.
(Your parents may have to sign with you or for you in
many areas if you are under eighteen.)

We've already mentioned that VCR tape rentals head
the list of teen purchases. Compact discs (CDs) are also
growing in popularity as the costs of both players and discs
come down. If you are getting into stereo equipment, do
some comparison shopping. Find a stereo with a good
manufacturer's warranty. Typical coverages would be:

• Speakers—3 to 5 years.
• Receiver, components, or tape deck—1 to 3 years.
• Turntable, headphones, equalizers—1 to 2 years.

Stores may or may not add their own satisfaction guarantee to a manufacturer's warranty. Look for such protection.
It means that if what you buy does not work "out of the
box," you can exchange it for a satisfactory unit right away.
It pays to ask before you buy.

Sales are so widespread in electronics, stereos, cameras,
and other popular products that it seems no one sells at
"list price." For this reason, you should forget so-called
manufacturer's suggested retail prices. Instead, comparison shop newspaper ads so that you wind up with the best
"sale" price for what you want. When comparing prices,
look for the best price on the brand name *and model number* of the product you want. (These numbers are often
listed in ads.)

Now that you've bought your bike/car/stereo/new

clothes, how do you pay? Charge card? Layaway? The age limit has been lowered by many credit card-issuing companies, and now young teens—especially those with savings accounts—may find Visa or MasterCard plastic in their pockets.

There's nothing wrong with credit cards if you budget the money to pay the bills when they come in. Smarter yet, you could send payment *ahead* of the bill, to save on interest charges (see Chapter 6 for details.)

Credit cards and charge accounts are very convenient. But they can also be a problem, as we have said. Young (and not-so-young) people often use the handy plastic and forget that one day they'll have to pay for what they purchased. Coping with credit cards and charge accounts can be quite a challenge. (Layaway plans may be a more satisfactory solution because you don't receive the item until it's paid for.)

Suppose you have a complaint with a product you have bought? If you purchased it by credit card and the merchant believes you have good reason to complain, the salesperson or store manager will exchange the item for one that works (if you can, test it in the store). If an exchange isn't possible, the store will arrange for a credit on your credit card account.

If you paid cash for an unsatisfactory item, in most cases you will also receive an exchange or a refund—if you have that all-important receipt.

But suppose you have trouble getting a refund for a product that doesn't satisfy you? If so, you enter the somewhat annoying area of customer complaints.

Here's the rundown on getting your money back:

- First of all, make sure your complaint goes to the right person. For instance, if a hair dryer doesn't work, see the salesperson who sold it to you or the head of the department in which it was purchased. If the salesperson won't help you, ask for his or her supervisor. If you still get stonewalled complain to the store's corporate headquarters.

- If you don't get satisfaction at this stage, or if the store's policy is to have complaints handled by the manufacturer, your complaint takes a new turn. You must now resort to writing or phoning the company that manufactured or distributed the product. (The address may be on the package or the instruction sheet.) If it is a large corporate office, check for a local or toll-free number. (Call 1-800-555-1212 for information on toll-free phone numbers.) If there is no toll-free number, you may decide to put your complaint on paper. Check in *Standard & Poor's Register of Corporations*, available at most libraries, to see if the address you need is listed.

- If you send your letter to the Complaint Department, it will probably find its way to the right source. Try to keep your letter short and to the point. Unless the instructions with the product tell you not to do so, send it back with your letter. Otherwise, give the product's model and serial numbers and describe its malfunction. Also, send copies of your sales receipt and credit card charge (if you used a card to make your purchase). Don't send the originals, for then you have no proof of purchase. You should now receive an answer and instructions about what to do to get your money back.

- If you are not satisfied with the company's action on your defective purchase, you can write to the Better Business Bureau office in your city or to your county or state department of consumer affairs.

Shoddy products and money problems can be worrisome, but they're part of life. A group of St. Paul, Minnesota, teenagers decided to cope with *other* people's money problems as a way of experiencing real-life situations. The students invited people in their town to use their Consumer Action Service. With the aid of lawyers, small claims courts, and other resources, the teens worked to help many residents solve serious money problems.

In one case, a woman complained that she had bought a used piano that didn't play properly. Even after a thorough tuning, the piano keys stuck and the tone quality was poor. The dealer refused to take the piano back.

The students determined that the dealer had not given the customer a fair deal, but since there was no contract involved in the sale, there was little she could do about it—a sad lesson for the buyer.

Other cases involved apartment disputes and faulty roof repair. As the students researched each case, they learned about things that could easily happen to them later in life.

The St. Paul students found out that it's a tough world out there! The money problems they and teenagers across the country face are quite different from these adult dilemmas—but spending money wisely enters the picture in both cases. How well you handle your money today can be a sign of how things will go in your financial future.

What TV ads appeal to you (so that you'd go out and buy the product) and what ones do you feel are "faking"?

Although I am not often influenced to buy from TV commercials, ads that make me think (usually with a clever ending statement) or are unusual appeal to me. Most automobile ads turn me off immediately, except for "Joe Isuzu" because it is unusual. Ads with flashing numbers, loud voices, and too much information (*e.g.*, Toyota ads) are not entertaining, and therefore turn me off. Ads that are obviously insulting to my intelligence (*e.g.*, Acme's Millie and Sandy (?)) make me turn the channel. Commercials designed like the MTV videos make me sick—they are cheap imitations.

—Matthew Oberholzer

TV ads for things like VCRs and stereo equipment and gold jewelry appeal to me. TV ads for things like cars and things that you get money back for seem kind of phony because I feel that if they are giving you money back, you'll probably end up paying more in the end.

—Melanie Bryant

I like ads that express artistic and clever sales pitches (i.e., Mercedes, BMW) although I am not ready to buy a car. I think that ads using cheap sex appeal are low class and real people don't act that way.

—Christopher Oberholzer

The Basics of Banking
and Credit

Are you important to a bank? The American Bankers Association thinks so. According to *U.S. News and World Report*, the A.B.A. conducts a personal economics program in high schools in nineteen states that has reached over 750,000 students since 1984. The news item quotes Mississippi banker William Sones: "We go into every high school in our county and, for one week a year, an hour a day, hold classes on how to balance a checkbook and use consumer credit."

Students in a Florida school recently carried all the rules of banking to their logical conclusion: They founded an actual bank. These student-bankers had the help of a real bank in drafting their charter. Their venture is legal; it is a branch of the parent bank.

Before starting their bank, the students spent months of part-time training with the sponsoring bank, which helped them as a community involvement project. To launch their bank, the students sold shares, to make other students into bank stockholders. The bank offers savings accounts to students of the participating school; other services are being added as the bankers gain experience.

Now that he has sampled this phase of adult life, one of the student board members sums it up as "complicated." While operating a bank may indeed be complicated, understanding how banks work and how to use their services is fairly straightforward.

A bank is any organization that offers money-related services and does so at a profit. Banks are of two basic types: savings banks and commercial banks. Both offer much the same services—savings (where your money earns money), checking (where your money may be transferred to someone else with a written promise on your part to pay), and loans (where you borrow money, are charged interest for using it, and repay in regular amounts).

A savings account is your logical starting point with the banking system, for two reasons. First, it's easier to get than a checking account. Second, it's more useful for you right now, although a checking account may be just the thing later on.

Walk into any bank, savings or commercial, and you'll see a display showing what percent interest that bank pays for various types of savings. These rates may go up or down, depending on a variety of economic factors that affect the value of money and the cost of borrowing. Competition among banks may make rates more attractive for the same type of savings—a passbook account, for instance —at one bank than at another.

The longer your money must stay on deposit and the less easy it is to withdraw your savings, the higher the rate of interest your money can earn. Also, the more money you can deposit in one *savings instrument*, as the banks call it, the better your rate of return will be and the more money your money will make.

DOCUMENTS HELD BY TEENAGERS

	National	Male	Female	Ages 13-15	Ages 16-17
Social Security card	78%	75%	80%	67%	94%
Library card	71	67	75	73	68
Driver's license or permit	37	37	38	10	80
Passport	10	11	9	8	14
Savings account	62	63	60	60	66
Checking account	10	11	10	8	14
Credit card	4	5	3	2	7
None of the above	4	5	3	5	1

Source: Gallup Youth Survey, 1987.

A passbook account pays the least interest but offers the most convenience. You can deposit any amount and withdraw what you want at any time. You may have to keep a certain amount of money (the *balance*) in your account, or use it fairly often, or both, to avoid paying the bank a charge for having an inactive account.

Savings certificates (also known as CDs or *certificates of deposit*) are available in different time periods, from months to years. You may need to save several hundred dollars to buy one (why not in your savings account?), and you may not cash in (*redeem*) a certificate ahead of its maturity date without paying a penalty—some loss of interest.

In shopping around for savings, you should look not only at the rate of interest paid (7.00 percent a year is obviously better than 6.25 percent) but also at the *effective annual yield*, which is almost always higher. It is higher because your interest will be *compounded*.

Here's how compounding works (take a deep breath!).
The interest rate (the 7.00 percent, say) is expressed in
simple interest. If you earned simple interest on $100 for
one year, $7 would be added. Compound interest is added
to your account more often than once a year. It can
be every six months (semiannually), every three months
(quarterly), even every week or every day.

In compounding, the interest earned by your money is
added to the money itself, and in turn this new total earns
interest. So the more often the interest is added to your
account to earn interest,the higher the effective annual
yield will be. Daily compounding produces the highest
yield, so when you compare banks' savings plans, compare
effective annual yields rather than interest rates and go for
the highest number available for the length of time you
want to invest your money.

Banks of all kinds pay interest on savings because they
want to have customers' money available to lend to others.
They charge more interest on loans than they pay on savings, so they make a profit. Just as savings rates differ from
bank to bank, not all financial institutions charge the same
rates for loans.

How do you start a savings account? You need only a few
dollars, and possibly a Social Security number. You may
open a checking account at some savings banks at any age
and in a commercial bank if you're eighteen or older.

In a checking account you deposit money by giving the
bank a deposit slip showing your account number and the
cash or checks that you wish to deposit. In turn, you write
checks against the amount in your account to people you
wish to pay. By writing a check, you promise that person
that the money actually exists in your account and may be
withdrawn by that person. That person withdraws from
your account by depositing your check in his or her

account. Your check then goes back to your bank, which credits the money you owe to that person's account.

When someone writes you a check, you collect the amount written on the check if you can get someone to cash it (not always easy) or if you deposit it in your own checking or savings account. In the latter case the check travels back through a *clearinghouse* (part of the Federal Reserve system) to the bank it came from, and that bank deducts the amount of the check from the writer's checking account. Not until then is the amount of the check credited to your account. That may take a week or longer—so don't spend money you *think* is in your account the minute you deposit someone's check in it!

If you need a checking account at all—and you may not for a few years—the best value is what many banks call a special checking account. With this account, you write only a few checks a month and can maintain a relatively small balance. You pay a few cents for writing each check, and you may also have to pay a small fee for each deposit you make. This type of checking account is popular with teens and others who don't need to write many checks.

A regular checking account is far more busy (*active*, in bank language). You may need to maintain a fairly large minimum balance. If your balance is large enough, you may not be charged for checking account services. If it is larger still, the bank may even pay some interest on it. As with every banking service, it pays to shop for checking accounts.

When you open a checking account, your credit history is checked through a central record-keeping bureau (this goes for credit cards, too). You probably do not yet have a credit history; this automatic check is made to weed out people who do have one—a not-so-good one.

A checking account can be misused, although doing so is

strictly against the law. Postdating checks (writing them with a date in the future), writing checks without the money in your account to cover them (kiting checks), or even writing checks that accidentally "bounce" and come back to you marked NSF (not sufficient funds) because you lost track of your balance are all banking no-no's that will damage your credit rating.

A checking account is your responsibility to keep in balance. You have to figure the cost of each check, each deposit (if they are charged for) and each monthly service charge. You have to keep an accurate record of the deposits you make and the checks you write. And each month (or each quarter, with certain low-activity special accounts) when your statement arrives from the bank, you have to *reconcile* it; that is, review your arithmetic against the bank's figures, to make sure neither of you has made any mistakes. A checking account may not be worth the trouble unless you find yourself running a small business where much of your money comes in the form of checks, or unless you have many people to pay. If you collect money in the form of checks but do not write many, you can deposit the checks in a savings account.

Two kinds of "plastic money" are available from most banks. One is easy to get—the "money machine" or ATM (automatic teller machine) card that lets you get cash from your account day or night at any machine in the network that accepts your bank's card. In addition to your name and your account number, you also need a secret *access number* that you memorize. This prevents anyone who finds your card from using it.

The other kind of "plastic"—a credit card—can be secured through a bank, but the agreement may have to be cosigned by your parents if you are under eighteen or until you have built up a credit history of your own. Even with your parents cosigning, you may have a relatively low charge limit (*line of credit*) to start with. (Two Philadelphia-area banks report a $300 limit; others require that a teen-ager be working full time to qualify for a credit card.)

Bank cards, department store credit cards, and those offered by oil companies for drivers' convenience have several elements in common. All offer credit limits that can be (and often are) raised for cardholders who pay on time—though you need not pay the full amount owed each month. They all charge interest, although not all cards of the same kind (such as Visa or MasterCard) charge the same interest rate. They may or may not offer interest-free "grace periods." And they usually but not always charge an annual fee.

That's the true credit card—a sort of "plastic loan." The other so-called credit card should really be called con-venience card. Such cards are issued by organizations such as American Express and Diners Club. There is a yearly charge of $35 to $50 but no credit limit. Interest is not charged unless you request extended payment. But you ordinarily must pay the balance in full within 30 days or less of the time you're billed.

You can see that credit cards can do a lot for you. You can buy expensive things without the danger involved in carry-ing cash. You can buy all kinds of things with a bank card such as Visa or MasterCard, since they are honored at thousands of locations. You can rent hotel rooms and cars and buy airline tickets, among other things. Credit cards are safe and convenient.

But credit cards can do a lot *to* you. It's very easy to buy things now for which you expect (or hope!) to earn the money later—then be hit with a big bill that you can't pay.

Department store and bank credit cards can add to your temptation. Let's say your credit limit is $300. You get a bill for $100 in purchases. But the bank or store will let you make a minimum payment of $5, $10, or at most $15 of the $100 for that month and you're still free to spend another $200! It's very easy to get into this sort of bind but not so easy to get out. The bank or store is delighted; it can keep on charging you interest on the unpaid balance—and you can keep on charging purchases until you reach your credit limit. Since there's nothing to hold you back but your own good sense, true credit cards can, and often do, become a real drag. But they are a fact of life, so the sooner you train yourself to use them well, the better.

After there good deals in cards, as in other banking services? Sometimes. Department and chain stores that issue credit cards set their interest rates and terms, and there's nothing you can do about them. Not so bank cards. Since interest rates and other conditions do vary, you can shop for such cards. You may have to take the first card you can get to begin with, but when that card comes up for its annual renewal you can look around to see if another bank offers a better deal.

Some bank cards charged a yearly fee, but not all charge the same fee. The interest rate (expressed as APR, *annual percentage rate*) may be lower at one bank than another, and the grace period may be longer, or there may be none. So look for a free card (at least for the first year's fee), a low APR, and a grace period. But whatever you do, read that pesky small print before you sign your credit card agreement, and try to understand it. Most such agreements are not written for easy understanding!

Credit cards may be a thing of the future for you—especially if your suggestion of parents' cosigning goes down with a thud. A checking account, too, is something you may not deal with for quite a while. But now that you know something about how these and other forms of banking and credit work, you will be better able to use them well when the time comes.

Do you have a savings account? A credit card? (Don't laugh—some kids do!)

I have two savings accounts, and presently I am waiting for investment certificate interest rates to rise before I invest some of these funds.

—Matthew Oberholzer

I don't have a savings account but I'm going to look into it because I feel that I need one. I'd love to have a credit card, but I don't think my mother would go for that idea.

—Melanie Bryant

I have a savings account and deposit often.

—Christopher Oberholzer

CHAPTER 7

Stocks and Bonds, Or How Your Money Can Make Money— Maybe

QUESTION: What goes up and down, and runs on
money?
ANSWER: The stock and bond market.

In schools across the country, more than 200,000 junior
high and high school students learn about the stock market
in the most direct way possible: by forming teams and
making their own investment decisions for ten weeks each
year.

Although each small team starts with $100,000 and cred-
it worth another $100,000, team members are not chil-
dren of the rich and famous—because every dollar invested

is imaginary. But every move in The Stock Market Game is absolutely real.

The ninth- and twelfth-grade student teams at Pennsylvania's Hatboro–Horsham School are typical of the young investors who read the stock quotations every day in the newspapers, devour financial articles in business journals, and then write out forms to make as many as fifty computer-recorded stock "buys" or "sells" a week. One ninth-grade team "made" $8,000 in nine weeks. If this rate had continued for a year, they would have earned a 50 percent return on their investment!

The rules of the game include being able to buy stocks on *margin* (buying the stocks on credit or with a small down payment, then selling them at a profit, paying the lender, and pocketing the difference) and *selling short* (a way to make money if the stock market goes *down*). Deductions must be made for the *brokerage fees* for buying and selling, for interest on borrowed money, and for other "real world" financial transactions.

Teams compete against each other to determine area winners—the teams that make the most money on their stock market activity during the ten weeks. Gains or losses are based on the actual ups and downs of real stocks. (Another Hatboro–Horsham team "bought" American Oil (Amoco) at $72 and "sold" it a few weeks later at $84, for a tidy $12 per share "profit" before expenses.) There is, of course, no guarantee that even the most talked-about "sure thing" will turn out the way it was predicted.

In each area of the country where it is played, The Stock Market Game is supported by regional stock exchanges, brokerage firms, and colleges. Wherever it is taught—usually in social studies or economics classes—the game has been praised for the practical yet exciting way it shows teenagers and their younger brothers and sisters how money can be made (and lost) on Wall Street, as the New York Stock Exchange is nicknamed.

If the game is not yet being played in your area, your friends and a teacher-sponsor may be able to form a team and join in the action. For information, write to Securities Industry Foundation for Economic Education, 120 Broadway, New York, NY 10271.

There are other ways to learn about high finance. The New York brokerage firm Shearson Lehman Hutton has helped establish the Institute for the Study of Finance. This unique organization includes programs that help prepare New York area high school students for investment careers. The Institute program includes two years of instruction plus summer jobs on Wall Street. Instruction covers financial accounting, how Wall Street operates, data processing, the basics of banking, the insurance industry, and financial planning.

Another financial learning experience was almost too successful. A group of junior high school students in Easton, Massachusetts, helped by a teacher, formed their own by-and-for-kids commercial bank. The idea was great— an easy, enjoyable way to learn about lending money and operating a bank for profit. Unfortunately, the idea was also illegal, according to state bank examiners. They stumbled across the students' "bank" when they routinely audited the real-life savings bank that had done the kids a favor by reviewing their proposal for accuracy. The examiners visited the school, then closed down the "bank" for operating without a $200,000 charter, charging too much interest on loans, making loans without a license, and using the word "bank" in their business name without authorization from the state. A life lesson, yes—but not quite the one the young bankers expected.

Although this venture did not succeed, there is no reason why you cannot invest in stocks, bonds, and other securities. There are no laws to prevent young people from "playing the market." But when the game is real, with your own money, you should know what you're going to do— and how to do it—before you make the plunge.

The following basic information may help you decide whether investing is for you. But there is so much to know about investing (and not just in the stock and bond market) that you should read some of the books listed in the Bibliography to increase your understanding before you begin.

The two most popular types of investments are *stocks* and *bonds*. Bonds are generally less risky than stocks. We'll discuss them first.

Where does the money come from to build schools, improve transit systems, expand power plants, and enlarge airports? Largely from *bond issues*, which are *floated* by cities, towns, and other municipal authorities. These bonds are expensive when compared to stocks, costing perhaps $1,000 each, or more. The money for design and construction is raised by the sale of these bonds. Since it may be ten or even twenty years before such bonds *mature* (when the bondholder is repaid), bonds pay a predetermined rate of interest each year until they mature. Both the interest and the eventual repayment come from school taxes, transit fares, utility bills, or airport user fees. Since it's not too likely that a city, school district, electric company, or airport will go out of business, your money is relatively safe. You can sell your bonds at any time if you don't wish to wait for maturity. You can also buy bonds from corporations and from the United States Treasury.

Stocks are riskier than bonds, but they generally earn more money. A share of stock is a share in a business; as a stockholder you become a part owner. (How would you like to say you own part of Toys R Us, or Walt Disney World?) If times are good and the business makes money, that company becomes more valuable in the eyes of other people. The dollar value of your share, or shares, will go up, because others will be eager to buy into such a fine corporation. And when business is good the company's board of directors may vote you a healthy *dividend*, or payment, every year. This can be in cash, in additional shares of stock, or both.

If, on the other hand, the company's business is not good, the stock dividend will be small, or may not be paid at all. If lots of investors see a corporation having trouble, the value of its stock will go down because many people who own the stock may try to sell it, but not many people will risk buying it. The price could fall below what you paid for it, and you would lose money if you sold it. Sometimes selling before things get worse is wise, but sometimes it's better to hold on and wait for the company to recover and the stock price to rise.

The *stock exchange* is the marketplace where most bonds, and nearly all important stocks, are traded. While the usual market offers products for sale, the busy stock exchange deals every day in thousands of numbers, indicating the prices of stocks and bonds being bought and sold. The value of a certain stock is a combination of supply and demand—what the buyers and sellers agree it's worth. This value can change hour by hour, depending on the acitivity and mood of the market in general, the state of the industry of which that company is a part, or the actions of company officers (any drastic change causes stock to rise or fall). *Stockbrokers* earn their living buying and selling investments for their customers, and advising them.

A *mutual fund* (sometimes called an *investment trust*) is

a good way for beginners to enter the market. It is a collection of stocks or bonds that are bought, sold, and managed by a group of investment specialists on behalf of the fund's customers. You buy shares of the fund, just as you would buy shares of IBM or Ford—but you leave the stock buying and selling decisions to the experts who operate the fund for you. There are different types of funds to meet different investor needs; some are more conservative, or safer, than others.

As a very general rule, the safer an investment, the less money it will make for you. Riskier investments tend to earn more money—but never use money for high-risk investments that you *cannot* afford to lose. There is, of course, no guarantee of safety or success anywhere in the stock or bond market, but some investments are definitely safer than others.

Some stocks and other investments are not listed on a major stock exchange or other securities market. These are often speculative—not for the inexperienced or the weak-kneed. If a speculative investment succeeds, it succeeds gloriously. If it fails, it fails spectacularly. Usually any investment that sounds too good to be true is exactly that.

Youngsters have earned as they've learned about investing. A Maryland financial planner helps his own two children to invest by setting aside 20 percent of their allowance for them to invest in companies they select—the fast-food restaurant they go to, and the soft drink they prefer, among others. As their stocks grow in value, this thoughtful father matches their earnings with equal dollars—but for their stock portfolios, not their pockets.

Other investors have started very young to make their own investment decisions. A hard-working California investor was just eleven when he began making important and profitable choices that surprised even his stockbroker.

This talented youngster, Stanley Martinez of Chula Vista, California, got interested at age six when someone gave him a book about money.

Another youthful investor turned his personal market wisdom into a mutual fund by the time he was a junior at Princeton University. Jim Lavelle's fund managed some $100,000 for seven clients—and he operated it from his dormitory room.

Four Florida hotels offered a summer camp for teen-agers and preteens, but instead of canoeing and hiking the students learned to understand *The Wall Street Journal* (finance's daily newspaper) and took courses in stocks, bonds, and personal finance. In its July 6, 1987, issue, *Insight* magazine reported, "For $500, Mom and Dad sun and sail while the kids receive investment advice from two...consultants." A $100-per-camper mutual fund was part of the program.

A final thought about investing—and this holds true whether you buy or sell stocks, bonds, mutual funds, real estate, gold, silver, or rare coins: You must pay federal taxes on your investment income just like an adult.

Under the recent changes in the tax laws, every child over the age of five needs a Social Security number for identification and so that his or her income can be properly recorded. No longer can you take a personal exemption for summer job earnings or investment income on your own income tax return (if you earn enough to have to file a return). If your parents declare you as a dependent and as an exemption on their tax return, as they probably would prefer, you will have to pay your share to the Internal Revenue Service. So as you earn, remember to put money aside to pay your share of income taxes every April 15, just like everyone else.

How to Earn Money

On Your Own

Although jobs in malls and shopping centers pay off, the greatest source of money is in or near your own backyard. When your two feet make the rounds of the neighborhood, you can come up with new ingenious ways to make money as well as profitt from the more traditional services. Jobs may range from mowing lawns and baby-sitting to staging a garage sale or acting as disc jockey for parties.

Some of the jobs you may do for family and neighbors are relatively easy to agree on. But many of them require a professional approach to convince your neighbors that you are capable of performing them. This professionalism may involve cleanly lettered or typed flyers, accurate bookkeeping, promptness—the whole package that makes you a marketable person.

The jobs you undertake may be short term—sweeping an occasional terrace—or long term—a washing/waxing service, for instance. You may not know exactly how you want to earn money. Sandra Froese, in a recent issue of

Seventeen magazine, suggests that you make lists of the things you are good at or like to do. Do you excel at sports? Do you get along with children? Are you good with tools? Do you like animals? Decide on your strong points. You will find that many of your "pluses" correspond to the money-making ideas described later in this chapter.

Another thing you can do, Ms. Froese notes, is make a plus-and-minus chart for what appeals to you. Example:

Caring for Pets
Pluses:
Like animals.
Hope to be a veterinarian.
Minuses:
Not allowed to bring neighbors' pets home.
May be away often this summer.

Baby-sitting
Pluses:
Like kids.
Baby-sit for younger sister so have experience.
Minuses:
Live far from families with children.
Can't always make kids behave.

Until you can get something going that you really like, your parents may be a source of earned income. They usually have endless things to be done that they can't get to themselves—ranging from repairing the fence to giving the dog a bath.

It is particularly important to be professional with parents. Agreements on fees and length of job time apply to them, too. Parents may tend to ignore these agreements because after all, you're their kids. Don't let them. On the other hand, you have to keep your part of the bargain, too.

Many of you are already employed outside the home. The most common jobs are baby-sitting for girls and lawn-mowing and newspaper delivery for boys. But the traditions of the male lawn-mower and female baby-sitter are giving way to girls doing lawn work and boys watching over the small fry. This is great! It gives a teen twice the number of job possibilities. Where is it written that girls can't shovel snow or paint houses and boys can't offer house-cleaning services? In fact, girls are strongly advised to seek boys' jobs because they are generally better paying. There's no job-limit, either, on the jobs you create yourself. If you make (and sell) a great batch of brownies, boy or girl, you profit. If you start a car-washing service, male or female, you will make money.

Before you tackle jobs outside the house, how do you negotiate for them? You may simply have an oral agreement with the people you work for or you may want to draw up an informal contract that sets your fee. A contract may be particularly important if you are starting a summer or seasonal business. If you intend to organize garage sales or start a disc jockey service, you will certainly want to put some rules on paper. These will protect you and your customers in case of misunderstandings.

Here is a simple contract to give you the idea:

(Your name) will baby-sit for (family's name) on Tuesday and Friday nights in July and August. (Family's name) will pay $ _____ on Friday of each week.

_____	_____
Your signature	Date
_____	_____
Family's signature	Date

Managing garage sales and conducting businesses such as a lawn-mowing service can be pinned down in similar terms.

You may also want to advertise your services. Adults are impressed by teenagers who have a written list of the services they can perform. Make sure to deliver your flyers to your neighbors. Also, pin them to supermarket and shopping mall bulletin boards. If there are apartment houses nearby, leave a stack of flyers near the mailboxes.

Many of the activities discussed in this chapter call for negotiated payments. If someone wants you to be a golf caddy or a gardener, you have to decide how much to charge. You can charge by the hour or set a flat fee. If you are not sure what to charge, find out what your friends might charge and decide from there. Also, make it clear ahead of time that you may ask for more money if the task takes longer than you expected. Tell people ahead of time that this may happen, especially on jobs you agree to do by the hour. What looks like a two-hour job may take three to do correctly.

So many ideas are listed here for making money that you need never be bored—or poor. See which ones appeal to you the most. If you choose jobs that you enjoy, you can make money doing things that are fun and rewarding.

Baby-sitting

Baby-sitting is a responsibility, but it is also a pleasure. You will be "rehired" by the kids rather than the parents, because little children are very loyal to a sitter they like. Boys are as popular for the job as girls. Small children like girls because they'll curl up endlessly and read to them, or bake cookies and pizza. Little children like boys because they feel they can climb all over them and roughhouse with them. This description may seem to stereotype boys and girls in their roles as baby-sitters, but small children often feel differently according to whether boys or girls are their caretakers. It doesn't mean girls won't give a great piggy-back ride or that boys won't enjoy reading a good book aloud.

Baby-sitting is a great responsibility because you have total care of the child or children. That's why it's always important to know safety rules. It couldn't hurt to know CPR, a life-saving technique, and to know where to locate an adult quickly should you have problems.

Some communities sponsor classes to help teenagers be effective baby-sitters. Check with the Red Cross or the public school health program to see if such a program exists.

You can baby-sit in the child's home or the child can be left at your home. There are advantages to both arrangements. Young children in their own home have all their things in familiar places and may feel more secure. Your house, on the other hand, may be a treat because it is full of new sights and pleasures. You, the children's parents, and the children themselves can decide where they will stay.

Once you have the job, what are you going to do with the kids? Babies, of course, are on a fairly rigid schedule so your work is really preplanned. But what of the two- to five-year-olds? You can sing songs, read books, and play simple games. Elementary school children are probably the easiest to care for because by that age they know what they want to do. They like television, playing with friends, and entertaining themselves with their own projects.

The Council on Family Health has some guidelines for the good baby-sitter:

- Be sure parents give you the address and telephone number where they can be reached.
- Ask about any problems that might come up and any activity, refrigerator snacks, or TV shows that are forbidden.
- Ask the hour for bedtime so that you don't have the children fooling you into a late curfew.
- Watch the children constantly, particularly when they are in the kitchen.
- Do not open the door to anyone other than those expected.
- If it is night, be sure some adult sees you home and watches to see that you get into your house.

How do you advertise your services? Generally, you don't have to. Every parent on the block (and for miles around) knows who is available for baby-sitting. The competition can be so fierce that many parents won't reveal the names of their sitters.

But if you are having trouble finding a job, you may need to scout out children and ask their parents if you may baby-sit for them. Also, ask your parents to tell their friends about your availability.

Find out what is the going rate if you're unsure what to charge for baby-sitting. There's no point in asking a lot more than your friends because you'll price yourself right out of a job—and if you charge less you may lose your friends.

Upper Moreland Township outside Philadelphia, Pennsylvania, offers baby-sitting courses for its preteen and teen residents. For over eight years, young people have been meeting on Saturday mornings to qualify for a baby-sitting certificate. This certificate puts them on an official call-list for the township—a list that is considered invaluable by

parents of small children. The certified students are
trained to be friendly but firm with their charges. They are
advised to carry a "baby-sitting kit" that includes crayons, a
bath toy, and emergency bandages. They are taught about
potential fire hazards, how to stop someone from choking,
and what to do in case of accident. With all these skills, it's
obvious that Upper Moreland Township young people will
be professional in their baby-sitting approach.

Maid Service

It may seem a long way from baby-sitting for neighbors'
children to taking care of a neighbor's house. But maid
service may very much appeal to families nearby. Next to
taking care of the children, a woman's (and a man's) heftiest
job is taking care of the house. And for working women
housework is particularly difficult.

You're no stranger to housework. You've been making
(and changing) your bed, cleaning up the kitchen, perhaps
dusting for as long as you can remember. Why not do it in
someone else's house and be paid for it?

You can also be a party-helper. Offer to help serve a
dinner party, clean up afterwards, or do both. You're
bound to get a recall on such a service because the hostess
will wonder how she ever did without you. (Her guests
may also make a mental note about your services.)

The best way to find maid-service or party-service jobs is
simply to visit your neighbors (telephone first) and make
specific suggestions on how you could be helpful. Be persistent. Try not to take a turn-down. Many people are
afraid to try new things. They may think a teenager will
add to the work load rather than reduce it. Home owners
may feel that it's easier to do it all themselves rather
than direct someone else. If you encounter objections like

these, explain that you will soon know the ropes and will give your clients *extra* time for themselves.

Running a Fair or "Swap" Meet

Another activity that may bring in money for yourself or for a charity is running a fair or "swap" meet. It is guaranteed to give everyone a good time, and it can raise a surprising amount of money.

Running such an event takes a lot of planning and help. The very friends who may spend money at your event may also give you a hand at setting it up. Also, if they want part of the profit or hope to make money for charity, they will have to help you produce a swarm of attendees on the big day. (The same techniques you use to get summer jobs can be used to promote your event.)

Don't be afraid to charge enough for the fun you offer. Your time and expenditures need to be compensated by a substantial cover charge.

Let's take the fair project first. You'll need helpers to collect entrance money, to collect at each activity, or both. Your friends can also circulate publicity.

Your backyard fair—or one possibly staged at a local playground with permission—can be anything you want it to be. It can include a magic show, a karate exhibition, a "fish pond." For the fish pond, you could have a section with gifts appropriate for small children, and another with items for your own age group. (Cut loose on your imagination to surprise—or horrify—your friends.) Customers should be charged extra for the fish pond. (Read more about it later in this chapter.) Such activities are not thrown together in a day. It takes planning to attract customers and have them go home satisfied.

A "swap" meet can have all the variety of a fair, depending on the items available for swapping. Get your friends to bring items in good condition that they no longer want and sell or trade them. The items to trade can include everything from sports equipment and hamster cages to beaded jewelry. Discarded clothes and overpriced or shabby items don't sell well.

A snack bar can add to the fair or "swap" profits. It can be manned by a volunteer with whom you share the proceeds) or by "honor-system" self-service.

Like a fair, a swap-meet needs preparation. You'll need to advertise widely to attract not only participants, but also customers who come to browse. One way to make it easy on yourself is to have participants in the event bring their own tables to display their wares.

Garage Sale

The garage sale is not too different from a swap-meet, the main difference being that the used items do not belong to you or your friends. You would run a garage sale for a neighbor, taking over the entire task of advertising, pricing the items, and dealing with the customers. Sara Riehm's book *The Teenage Entrepreneur* is among several books that tell you how to do what millions of Americans are doing across the country—run a garage sale.

Many more people would like to run a garage sale but groan at the thought of the work involved. That is where you come in. You can help your neighbors get rid of the headboard that's been sitting in the attic for twenty-five years or the chipped china set.

Let's say you have found several neighbors who have agreed to have you manage a garage sale for them. Here are some tips:

- Agree with the owner or owners on the amount of pay you will receive. Whatever is decided upon should be firm whether the owner makes a profit or not.
- Check with community authorities on garage-sale permits (permission to put signs up directing customers to the sale). You may need one.
- Make or buy garage sale signs. You'll need large signs stuck into the lawn or on a part of the house visible to the street. You'll also need small ones to put on street corners as advertising and to direct customers to the sale.
- Have the owners price the items to be sold, or you can do it with them. Generally, used items in good condition sell at about half their original cost. (By the end of the day, however, your neighbor may tell you to knock down everything by another 20 percent.) You can buy small blank price stickers that peel off easily.
- Keep an eye on "the cookie jar"! That is, don't let the cash box out of your sight. Why? Because while you're helping a customer decide if a rickety chair will collapse if he sits on it, someone else may help himself to the day's profits. Keep cash out of sight, or carry it with you.
- Finally, help the owners clean up and put away the items not sold. (And try not to cut your profit by buying things left over from the sale!)

Disc Jockeying

The Kids' Money Book by Patricia Byers has lots of money-earning ideas. One of the most exciting ones involves disc jockeying for parties and proms, and your best customers may be your friends.

When your friends want to give a party (with or without dancing), or your class is looking for entertainment for the senior prom, you may be just the person to contact. The fee for this service can vary. Be flexible. Your friends may not have the financial resources that your school can offer for an official function. Simply charge according to what people can pay.

Disc jockeying is a bring-your-own project. You'll need a good, medium- to high-wattage stereo system, a microphone—and, of course, records. You'll also need a stereo turntable, or two, or one turntable and one tape deck. You may also want an assistant to help with all the equipment. Together, you should check out the system several hours ahead of time so there are no glitches when the party begins.

It's obvious that your record choices will be whatever you and your friends consider hot at the moment. If you don't have enough records of your own, borrow some from a friend. Just be sure you treat them with care. If you damage one, you'll have to replace it, and that would certainly reduce your profits.

You can offer your disc jockey services in three- or four-hour blocks. Take a ten-minute break every hour. This rest period will give you the energy to give the guests another lively session.

Spinning records is not your total job. You need a lively presentation to be a good disc jockey. You need to introduce your records and maybe make some appropriate comment at the end of each cut. This talk-along is also called "rapping" or "patter." It entertains your guests and adds continuity to your presentation. It takes practice to make your approach appear effortless. (Not all disc jockeys offer commentary; many simply play records.)

Car-Washing

What do you need besides a bucket, soap, rags, and water to get into the car-washing business? A partner or two—and some know-how about doing the job.

With professional car washes charging something like $5 per car for washing alone (hot wax is extra), you should learn to make very good use of your time if you plan to compete. A competitive price would be $4 for a wash and inside vacuuming. If two of you can do the job in 30 minutes, you each make the equivalent of $4 an hour—not too bad.

Your customer can enjoy certain benefits with your customized service. You should promote these services heavily in the flyers and newspaper ads you use to advertise your business. Promote the fact that the car is washed at the customer's home, with no need to line up at the car wash. It's washed at the same time every week, or every other week (always call first to be sure the customer and the car will be at home).

It's easy to learn how to perform a fast fluids check: motor oil, automatic transmission fluid level (caution: some cars must be operated to test this), radiator coolant reservoir, power steering pump—a reassuring "extra" you can offer that the car wash can't. It's certainly worth an extra 50¢ or 75¢ per car. (Be sure you're an expert in this service before you offer it to your customers.)

Waxing cars is another matter altogether. Professional "detailers" get $25 or more for a paste waxing and even more if the paint must be pretreated with a finished restorer. If you want to offer waxing services, experiment with the family car first. Some waxes and preparations are easier to use than others. (Some people have had good luck with one-step silicone-based preparations. On the other hand, a recently introduced wipe-on finish restorer from a well-known maker of auto waxes proved totally unsatisfactory.) As a general rule, if it's something you don't polish to a luster, don't try it.

Washing a car isn't as intricate, but it has its own distinct pattern, and if you do it this way you'll produce a good job in the shortest possible time:

Rule one: Have everything you need on hand, preferably in your own car, when you visit the customer's home. This should include a vacuum with a tool suitable for car seats, rugs, and headliner and possibly an extension cord. Carry your own hose and nozzle, bucket, mild detergent designed especially for car-washing, sponge or soft cloths, towels for drying, and a genuine chamois-skin (a good, big one) for final drying. Also, a spray type of leather and vinyl cleaner and a window cleaner with ammonia (or plain cider vinegar, a great grease-cutter that won't streak).

Rule two: Do the interior first, starting with the glass, which should be sprayed, wiped dry with paper towels, then finish-wiped with a cloth to remove spots. If you've been asked to use a product to clean or protect vinyl, do it now. Spray it on a paper towel, not directly on the surface, to avoid overspraying. Polish to a luster. Then vacuum the whole interior; carpets should be done last. Remove any protective mats and vacuum them (or even beat them with a stick) well away from the car. Vacuum under them, then put them back. End of interior.

Rule three: Use car-washing solution sparingly in a full bucket of warm water. Wash the car from the bottom up. If this sounds strange, consider: If you start from the top, the dirty water running down the sides will leave streaks. Do one half up to the window line, then the other half, then the front and the back. Hose this work down repeatedly as you go. If you're a team of two, one can wash as the other hoses down.

Rule four: Dry twice—again, teamwork speeds the job. Dry the roof first, using terry towels (dryer #1) followed by the chamois (dryer #2), which will pick up the last little bits of water left by the towels and give the paint and glass a bit of polishing in the bargain. Work your way down in the reverse order of the washing.

Rule five: Do the wheels and tires last. Do not use the hose. Instead fill your bucket with clear water—no soap. With a cloth, wash wheels and tires thoroughly. If the car has white sidewall tires, use a one-step liquid whitener on a cloth—do not use a stiff brush on whitewalls, since it will eventually scuff them and make them harder to clean. Rinse the wheels and tires well with another bucket and cloths—using the hose would splash the car. Dry with clean cloths, but do not use the chamois for this operation. The black of the tires will discolor it.

How do you know if the car you are washing needs a wax job? If you notice that your water runs off in flat sheets, the car could stand a waxing. If the water forms into beads as you wash the car, the finish is protected. If you do offer waxing, a reasonably bright paint finish will probably need one application of a one-step product. That's an hour's work for two, and worth $10 to $15. A dull finish will need a prewax cleaning, something of a hard job, followed by either a one-step protector or a conventional paste wax. Before you ever wax or spruce up a car's exterior, a complete washing is absolutely essential.

Once you have washed the car, look for things to point out to the owner, such as stone nicks, tar spots, and dents.

You may also be able to touch up the first and remove the second—for an additional fee, of course!

Repair Shop

Are you handy with tools? Do you often take mechanical things apart and find you understand the logic of how they work. And, better yet, do you get them back together again? If so, a repair shop may be a good money-maker for you.

If it's in a corner of the family garage or basement, your repair business can operate any time. You'll have to do a bit of promotion to get things going because repair customers aren't likely to be repeat customers. However, if you ask them to tell others about the service you offer, you may find your business growing.

What things can you repair with basic tools, mechanical ability, and common sense? Bicycles are a good bet, especially the one-speeds. Ten- and 12-speed bikes are a step up in complexity. And because of the intricate rear hub and the hand shift, the Sturmey-Archer type of three-speed bike is possibly the most temperamental of all. If you're really serious about bike repair, you may want to invest in a "how-to" book on the subject. However, much of bike repair is just common sense and tinkering.

The bike repair tools are relatively simple: a set of smaller-size metric wrenches, an all-in-one bike wrench, small slot-headed and Phillips-head screwdrivers, light-bodied lubricant, and a spoke tightener for trueing wheel rims. Last, but hardly least: a puncture patching kit.

Other likely repair jobs include small electric appliances (if an electrical supply house is handy for replacement parts), electrical fixture rewiring (lamp parts are available at any Kmart), gasoline-power appliances such as chain saws and lawn mowers—but *only if you know electrical wiring or engine innards and troubleshooting very well,* and repairing and refinishing children's scooters, small bikes, wagons, and such.

Often items are discarded that need only a little repairing to be made serviceable—and salable. You could expand a repair business to include collecting discarded items, fixing those that are fixable and selling them. Sales can be made through inexpensive ads in sell-and-swap newspapers, supermarket and other bulletin board announcements, and classified ads in your local weekly or neighborhood newspaper.

Although not strictly repair services, inside or outside housepainting, window-cleaning, and calking can be money-earners. If any of these involve climbing or the use of ladders, be sure you take your safety into account.

Lawn-mowing

Many young people (and this includes girls) find lawn-mowing an especially good way to earn steady money from May to as late as October. You can work singly or as part of a team. Someone will have to be of driving age and have a car available for all the equipment.

You'll need a power lawn mower you can depend on, one that's the right size for the lawns you will be cutting and one that you know how to use. It's possible to use a customer's lawn mower but better overall to have your own. If "your own" is really your parents', it should be your job to keep it gassed, oiled, and maintained. Also, if something breaks, you—not your folks—should have it fixed.

Professional lawn care teams will be out there trying to sell their services (at very inflated prices), so you should get your service rolling early in the spring. Advertise on supermarket bulletin boards and in local newspapers, and even print and distribute your own flyers door-to-door. Be sure any advertising includes a phone number where you can be reached.

Pricing is tricky. You'll have to price your services according to the going rate for your age group. Price by the lawn, not by the hour.

But price isn't everything. Reliability counts for a lot with customers. It pays dividends if you set the same day each week for cutting a given customer's lawn and then stick to it. Depending on where you live, you may have to allow for a rainy day or so each week, so don't book every hour of every day or you'll find yourself getting off schedule. Also, have it clearly understood that you're to be paid when you finish each cutting; you must be business-like yet polite about collecting.

Make sure ahead of time exactly what services you will perform for every customer. If lawn edging is part of the cutting, or weed-eating is done every other time, make sure you keep all these things straight. (These are extra-charge items, of course.)

A professional attitude comes just behind reliability in the operation of a successful lawn-mowing service. You're on trial when you do the first job for a new customer; he or she isn't obligated to continue with you if the work is incomplete or if your team is noisy, poky, or impolite. Never forget, you're in a *service* business.

It's a good idea to have your customer check out the first job you do. He or she can tell you if there are areas you missed or parts of the job that should be done differently. (A typical complaint might be that the lawn is not cut short enough. In that case, the lawn mower blade may need to be lowered.) Asking your customer to check your work will show that you care about what you do and help you keep your business all season.

While lawn-mowing alone is an excellent money-maker, you may wish to add plant watering, weeding, and simple pruning. Later you can offer leaf-raking, wood cutting, and, weather permitting, snow removal. Or if you live in the Sunbelt you may simply go on cutting lawns the year round.

It never hurts to let your lawn-mowing customers know you're available for odd jobs such as furniture moving, window cleaning, and such—especially if the lawns in your area take half the year off. In fact you probably won't need to tell your customers that you're free to do other things. You'll find them asking you to lift furniture or scrape terraces on an "off" day.

Golf Caddying

Caddying—carrying golf clubs for players—requires experience. You need to know the golf course and be familiar with all the clubs so that you can pull out the right one on demand.

A good caddy is also one who has an interest in the game. If you understand and enjoy golf yourself, your long hours on the course will be more enjoyable.

The hours may be irregular. Obviously, there will be lots of caddying in the summer, especially on weekends, when players may be out from sunup to sunset. Summer weekdays may not be so busy, and play will taper off if the winters are cold where you live.

How long does each game take? An eighteen-hole game can run from two to four hours. Of course the larger the group playing, the longer the game will take. If you're the easygoing type, their pace will probably be your pace. If you're an impatient person, you'll soon learn to relax, soak up the sun, and watch balls fly into sandtraps.

Caddying rates quoted here represent the average of several golf courses. They apply only to boys—more about girl caddies later. Boys are often rated A, B, or C caddies, based on experience. The A caddies may earn $45 to $55 a day; Bs, $40-plus; Cs, somewhat less. As caddies gain experience (and as certain caddies are requested by players), their ranking rises.

On "cart days" when everyone wants to be driven around the course, the earnings may be a bit less per 18-hole round. But you may be able to work an extra round, to your financial gain.

Caddying is a great job for boys, less so for girls. Not every club takes girls, and girls usually carry only one set of clubs, not the two sets a male caddy traditionally handles. Therefore, girls earn less in fees and tips than boys. Nevertheless, girls do caddy. It's simply a matter of finding a private club or public course that will accept them.

Recycling Aluminum, Paper, and Bottles

Each year more aluminum cans are collected as charities, fund-raising groups, and individuals discover the money potential of recycling. In 1987 some 35 billion aluminum cans were delivered to collection centers. Many of these make it back to store shelves and vending machines, whistle-clean, within twenty days of pickup. Also, recycling laws in some parts of the country involve very good payment for the return of used cans and glass bottles.

Recycling also extends the life of municipal landfills, fights litter, and creates jobs. Thirty thousand new jobs have opened up at recycling centers, aluminum companies, railroads and trucking firms, and makers of can-processing equipment. Recycling saves 95 percent of the energy it takes to make a new item. Recycling gives you more than money. You are collecting valuable resources to be used again, and you are also reducing the trash level.

You can share in this recycle mania, but to make money you have to be willing to lift, lug, sort, and deliver endless unwanted items. If you put method into this madness, you will find that it pays off.

You can learn where recycling centers are through your local newspaper, by word of mouth, or in the Yellow Pages phone book under Recycling Centers.

You make your money by the pound-weight of your materials. Twenty 12-ounce aluminum cans make a pound. As for newspapers, you'll soon learn to figure your poundage by casting an experienced eye at the height of your pile. Your final profit, then, will depend on how much effort you put into the project and the going rates for recyclable materials. These basic facts should make recycling less of a hit-or-miss money project.

Start, then, with your neighbors. Ask them to store recyclables for you to pick up once a week. Plan a route that keeps you from backtracking. Have plenty of boxes and large plastic trash bags in which to store the leftover loot. Your neighbors probably won't ask for payment because (1) you're doing them a service; and (2) it would drastically reduce your profit.

A group of Philadephia students collected 150,000 bottles for a school project. That's 15,000 pounds, or seven and a half tons of bottles. The students were rewarded with two free baseball tickets for every 500 bottles they turned in.

The collection started as a science assignment at St.

Gabriel's School, and other schools joined the effort. The project was two-pronged: It got bottles off littered streets, and it gave students a chance to attack the assignment in a variety of ways. One student, Bill Mosetter, collected 3,590 bottles by making the rounds of soda-and-snack shops.

Recycling Enterprisers, Inc. of Berlin, New Jersey, was the recipient of St. Gabriel's efforts. The company accepted twenty barrels of bottles at a time, giving the students ultimately over $50 a ton.

Charities and community restoration groups often make money by recycling products. Concerned citizens support everything from saving the whales to the Special Olympics by collecting discarded cans. In Texas recently businesses and private citizens went on a collection rampage to save the battleship *Texas*. The *Texas* had fought in two world wars and was slowly disintegrating. Now, thanks to an intense and dedicated interest in its survival, the ship will be living history.

Although you may not be trying to save a battleship, this story shows that the humble tin can can produce a profound effect. Or, for you—some pocket money.

Dog Bathing, Dog Exercising, and Pet-sitting Services

Note that we said "dog bathing service," not dog and cat bathing service. Can you imagine bathing a cat? First off, you'd get clawed and spat at. Second, they do a good job keeping themselves clean.

Dogs are a different story. Although they don't generally enjoy being bathed, they do tolerate a sudsy dip. And in most cases, they need it. Here are a few bath-facts about dogs:

- Although dogs don't sweat, they do get dirty. An occasional bath is necessary.
- Place a ring of suds around the dog's neck to keep the fleas in that area. Otherwise they will jump up into the dog's eyes and ears as you scrub. This sudsy ring will keep them in one place, to be scrubbed away at the end.
- When the dog is soaped, rinse it off, drain the old bath water, and rinse all the soap off with clean running water.
- Dogs won't catch cold after a bath if you give them a good toweling and let them run about. Then you can brush them to get a bright, glossy coat.
- Many dogs come to enjoy a bath as they bask in your attention.

If you are adept at dog-bathing, you might become very popular among your dog-owning neighbors. Few people really enjoy bathing their pets.

When you get a customer, prepare the tub at the owner's home, arming yourself with lots of old bath towels. (If the dog is big, you may need some help from a friend. The owner's presence will help to calm the dog, so be sure he or she stays on the scene.)

Reva Faver of Venice, California, has washed quite a few dogs in her time. She started out as a dog washer for a veterinarian when she was seventeen and now has a full-time business shampooing members of the canine world.

If you start a dog-washing business you probably do not plan to go into it with Miss Faver's intensity. On the other hand, her experience is interesting and may be helpful.

Miss Faver's "dogramat" is a do-it-yourself emporium where owners bathe their own pets. She comments: "I saw a great need for a place where people could groom their dogs at a minimal cost. They can also keep their project from becoming a battlefield between pet and owner."

At Miss Faver's dogramat, the four-legged customers sit in stainless steel tubs on wooden boards so they won't slip. After the owner washes and rinses the animal, hair dryers are available to dry and fluff out the coat. (Compare this to a garden-hose bath in the backyard!)

The dogs love to come to the dogramat and enjoy the attention from their owners. This is in sharp contrast to a bath-visit to the veterinarian's. "Dogs equate the vet's office with pain," says Miss Faver. "A dog may get a shampoo, but it also may receive an inoculation and other uncomfortable procedures. A dog that comes to Jaxon's dogramat (named for Miss Faver's German shepherd) knows he is coming for one reason: a warm, friendly bath."

Miss Faver's rules for dog-bathing are simple: a friendly atmosphere, lots of attention, and a comfortable bath temperature. You can apply these tips to your dog-washing service.

Dogs are supposedly man's—and woman's—best friends until they are deserted for the office or, worse yet, for vacations. Then they can become problems. Mildred Grenier, author of *How Kids Can Earn Cash*, says that young people can earn good money from animal owners because such people are hostages to their pets. Fido can't feed himself or get an airing, so someone must see to his needs. The Irish setter down the street is miserable unless she can remain in her own home—no kennel for her!

You most likely know the people who own animals in your neighborhood. Drop by and ask them to keep you in mind for dog-walking if they plan to go on vacation.

The smart teen in search of pet-exercise work can walk

two dogs, from the same household or not, and earn twice the money for the time spent. Just be sure your charges behave or they may walk *you*. (It's best to give the dog a trial walk while its owner is still around.)

Pet-sitting is related to dog-walking because it usually involves plenty of leash-time. Cats join dogs here because they too must be fed and perhaps let out. (Don't ever try to walk a cat on a leash—you will only get feline contempt for your efforts.

Pet-sitting is very popular with busy people because they prefer to keep their animals in familiar surroundings. Dogs and cats returning from week-long stays at a kennel or vet's often suffer "re-entry" problems. They may also bring back a few fleas. A pet left at home alone may be lonely but at least it's in familiar surroundings.

Your visits can break the loneliness for the household pet. Some gentle rough-housing will give your animal the exercise it needs. Unless you're told otherwise, morning and after-school visits for food and walking are probably needed for dogs; cats may be fine with one drop-in a day.

Whatever the pet owner can tell you about the animal's needs, interests, and habits will add to your service's success. The animal owner should let you know:

- When to water and feed the pet.
- Where the animal's food is kept, and how much to serve.
- Where leashes, litter box, toys, and treats are kept.
- The name of the veterinarian in case the animal becomes sick or appears lethargic.
- Any unusual habits or potential dangers (a dog that bolts and runs off if the front door is left open, or a cat that is not allowed outdoors).

The owner will give you a housekey so you can let yourself in and out. And incidentally, be sure that the pet you're caring for *wants* you to let yourself in. You should have little trouble with cats (the vicious attack cat is a myth!), but dogs are a different story. They can be quite unfriendly if the master or mistress is not around to supervise their behavior. Even a dog that you know well may consider you an intruder if you unlock the door yourself. The answer is to let yourself in with the key several times while the owner is still there but not in sight, to be sure the animal will behave when you're in charge.

Don't undercharge because you feel the job is an easy one. You're doing the pet owner a valuable service because he has few alternatives. He either boards the pet, which is expensive, or takes it with him, which is inconvenient if not impossible. So go ahead and charge a fair price for a specialty service.

Newspaper Delivery

How has almost every teen and preteen earned money at one time or another? Most teens have taken on a newspaper route at some point in their lives, and many continue to deliver papers until after-school activities make a route impractical.

What is it like to have a newspaper route? For one thing, it's a job with challenges. It's particularly challenging on rainy or snowy days, with newspapers blowing out of your bike basket or weighing down your shoulder sack. And collecting can often be a difficult part of the job. "I'll pay you next time" becomes a familiar put-off.

Contact the circulation manager of your local newspaper to secure a paper route. He or she will let you know where your paper pick-up is and will give you a list of your customers. You will find that the paper pick-up is a popular place—other young people will be picking up the papers for their routes. This daily get-together is a good way to make new friends. When the paper truck is late you have plenty of time for chatter, or tossing a ball around. (It's definitely an equal opportunity job; many girls as well as boys deliver newspapers.)

Some newspapers provide special incentives to attract paper carriers. Picnics, amusement park get-togethers, and cash bonuses (for staying with the route for a certain length of time and for getting new customers) are often part of the delivery job.

There's publicity, too. The *Montgomery County Record* serving suburban towns near Philadelphia highlights its paper carriers with pictures and quarter-page writeups. Most of these features reveal energetic young people who are able to fit paper delivery into their busy school schedules.

Giving Children's Parties

Many busy parents have turned to fast-food places to hold their children's birthday parties. Others still give parties at home but find themselves exhausted from the nonstop noise, occasional squabbling, and endless energy of a bunch of little kids. And then there's the clean-up after the party's over.

You can help these parents avoid the impersonality of a restaurant party or the exhaustion of running a party at home by offering a birthday party service (or Valentine's party, Hallowe'en party, etc.). By taking over the parents' responsibilities in their own home, you give the child the comfort of familiar surroundings and the parents can enjoy the festivities without lifting a finger.

It's best to run a party service with a friend. You may find you need moral—and physical—support. Your friend can help:

- When you break up a fight over who's going to play with a toy.
- When fruit juice is spilled all over the paper tablecover.
- When the kids get a sudden energy boost from the ice cream and cake (always serve the party food just before the *end* of the party!).
- When the children are gone, and the floor is knee-deep in wrappings and discarded toys.

Seriously, it's not as bad as all that. The secret is to plan every party step ahead. Planning can make a party run smoothly. For instance, a disagreement among the guests is less likely to erupt if the activities planned are lively and fast-paced.

You can plan the whole party, or you can accept the parents' suggestions. A mother may be delighted to give you full responsibility; on the other hand, she may want you to direct a game or activity that she considers traditional and fun.

What's the profit in an activity like this? Ten dollars would be a fair amount for all your work—more if you buy the prizes and birthday decorations and put them up. And even more than that if you bake the cake or make other party food.

How do you fill up those hours before the birthday cake arrives? You can play games such as the traditional pin-the-tail-on-the-donkey or plan newer entertainment such as renting a movie (assuming the parents have a VCR). Other activities might include outside entertainment like a magic show or clown act. If you have friends who are entertainers, they could appear as part of the party format. Or if you're talented in these ways, you could entertain alone or with a friend. Parents would understand that you would charge more if you import talent or are part of the act yourself.

You can also ask nursery school and kindergarten teachers for party ideas. Day-care centers provide entertainment nearly every day of the year, so their staff are full of ideas for young children.

Of course, you can keep kids going forever on the old favorites. They never tire of tag, hide-and-seek, and "Simon says."

One activity that is a crowd-pleaser is the "fish pond" where children dangle a string with a hook over a curtain and catch a gift. (Again, gifts for a fish pond would be added to the price of your party.)

To set up a fish pond, simply thumbtack a sheet across a door-way somewhat higher than the tallest child's head. The sheet can be decorated with paper fish that you have cut out and pinned to the cloth. Attach a string and a paper-clip "hook" to a short stick, and your party kids are all set to fish. When the child tosses the end of the line over the top of the cloth, you attach a beribboned gift to the hook.

Another activity full of suspense is a spiderweb treasure hunt. When done outdoors, each child follows a string around the yard that has been devilishly designed to twist through bushes, fences, and other kids' strings. Scale the complexity of your string trail to the ages of your party guests. Give each child a wooden clothespin to wind the string around as he or she reduces the distance to the surprise at the end (a toy or prize).

If there's rain in the forecast or you live in the city, you can spin the web indoors just as well. It can be just as lively in a twentieth-floor apartment as in any country setting. You will have to remove vases, ashtrays, knicknacks—all the breakables—before the party, so someone will have to entertain the party-child while you spin your web. And parents will probably stay out of the way because they will not *believe* what is happening to their house!

Another time-passer is the silly-artist game. Each child puts a piece of paper on his or her head and tries to draw a face on it. Because the children are unable to see what they're doing, the results are a riot. The kids may want you to do it, too—so be prepared!

Clean-up can be the most important part of the party in the parents' minds. They've paid you a good sum to run a birthday party. Their ultimate reward is that the place is restored to its original sanity. So look for every spilled gob of ice cream, every piece of gooey cake icing, and you'll find that the look of appreciation on the parents' faces is almost as rewarding as the cash you take home.

Gardening

Garden care and weeding may not instantly appeal as money-makers if you deal with these chores at home. Often, though, work done off the old plantation is much more pleasant—and the pay offsets some of the dreariness of the work.

So weeding and hoeing a garden plot may be worthwhile activities, especially when good money is involved. And the sheer gratefulness of the homeowner may be added reward. Your customers may be willing to do *anything* to get out of pulling weeds and cultivating between rows of vegetables.

Your employer should supply you with a trowel, rake,

hoe, clean-up plastic bags, and all the gardening paraphernalia. He or she should also explain carefully what is to be done. You don't want to mistake a flower bulb for a weed. Also, this is definitely by-the-hour work, because thorough weeding is a time-consuming job.

If you have had some experience with planting flower beds and tending rose gardens, you can suggest more ambitious plans to your employer. He or she might be open to some modest landscaping, edging of paths, or having you plan a rock garden, plant a flower cutting garden, or grow vegetables. If you're successful, you can expect to be invited back the next summer to repeat your green thumb act or to expand your tasks.

Gardening, like lawn-mowing, calls for regular appearances for weeding, watering, and perhaps treating plants against insects. Even if there isn't much to do on each visit (especially in mid- to late summer, when the weeds slow down), regular trips will help you keep each customer's garden under control—and keep your summer money-earning on schedule, too.

Painting

Home is the best place to learn housepainting and how to do interior trim and walls. If you have successfully painted windows without slopping paint on the glass or having the windows stick shut, then move on to trim, siding, terraces, shutters, gutters, and decks. When you've conquered these skills, you can confidently offer your services around your neighborhood.

Outdoor painting can be done whenever the temperature is over 50°F and rain is not forecast. Indoor work can be done year-round. As obvious as some of the following tips may seem, they're often ignored—even by adults—in their effort to get the job done. Never forget, it takes time to paint well.

Terraces, trim, fences, garage doors, and patio furniture all have a common denominator when it comes to painting: preparing the surface. Surface preparation can be a boring job. You can make it easier by being sure that you have a sharp, effective scraper. You apply this to all flaking areas, and if the surface has been painted many times you can expect to scrape away for a considerable time. If you're experienced, you can save time by using a belt or circular sander as well as hand-scraping. You will probably have to do further sanding and finishing to get a smooth surface, because paint does not hide flaws. Gather up the scrapings and dirt with a broom and dustpan or a shop vacuum.

Your customer will usually supply the paint and painting materials. If you are going to use a ladder, check it for safety—and be sure you have your parents' permission to do this sort of work. Always put drop cloths under where you'll be painting. If you're doing meticulous work such as window moldings or where two colors join, you may need masking tape to keep the work neat; sometimes a hand-held masking bar will do the job.

If you have a substantial area to cover, you can use a wide brush or roller, as well as sash and trim brushes for the small areas. Count on your paint job to take a bit of time. Because you don't know exactly how long it will take, it's probably best to charge by the hour. If you put a "ballpark" estimate on a terrace, for instance, and it needs more scraping than you counted on or a second coat you didn't expect, you will surely regret undercharging.

When you have finished your paint job, ask your customer how you should leave the painting equipment. If you have used an oil-based paint, soak brushes in turpentine or solvent, then dry them thoroughly on old rags.

Implements used for latex (water-based) paints should be thoroughly washed in soap and water, then dried. Cans of paint should be tightly sealed so the remaining paint won't dry out. A good paint job and a careful cleanup should be worth several referrals from satisfied customers—so be sure to ask for them.

Later on, if you go to college and have your summers open, your housepainting skills can become very rewarding. Many painters need experienced help in the warm months when housepainting is best done. (There's a very busy group of housepainters named College Pro Painters, and similar groups of student-housepainters probably work in other parts of the country.)

Cleaning Cellars and Attics

People will clean their cellars and attics, storage closets, and garages only when they have exhausted every possible excuse to avoid this tedious chore. Not only is the job messy and dusty, but it involves decisions. What shall I keep? What shall I toss away? Do I give away or junk the old lawn mower? The new one might break and I could resuscitate the old relic. (This is what you call tortured thinking.)

You will not be able to tell customers what to save and what to throw out, but you can be available for them as they make decisions. You can carry cartons, put similar items together, and in general serve as moral support for your beleaguered customer. He or she will surely want to do some sorting and throwing out before you clean the attic, cellar, or other space.

One way to sort unknown quantities of material is to move everything outside or into the open part of the garage and spread it out so it can be seen, checked for condition, and put in "keep" and "toss" sections. Meanwhile, you can clean the area where the things came from.

If you can clean an attic, you can clean a basement, and vice versa. All storage areas have one thing in common: mass confusion. Basements may have added problems of dampness and mold; attics and garages may be dusty and full of cobwebs.

Cleaning materials, then, should include such equipment as vacuum cleaner (the heavier duty, the better), brooms, and pails. You also may need strong detergents and dust rags.

A warning on this kind of cleaning: You may be like the person who paints himself into a corner and can't get out of the room. If you do not remove items so their future may be decided, you must be careful not to rearrange them in ways that make them hard to reach—or that make it hard for you to reach the exit. Before you clean, make good mental notes or do a paper plan lining up all the items to go back in storage in well-spaced rows. Clean areas in large blocks, or squares, then replace the items stationed there, or put others in their place. And be sure your customers know where you've placed what. A good idea in this department is to label every covered box with its contents.

A clean attic or cellar is not necessarily a place of beauty. But if it has a nice, clean smell and the contents are shipshape and findable, your customers will have got their money's worth.

And what is *your* money's worth in this venture? You can count on your project taking a full day, and possibly a weekend. A messy basement or attic is no feather-duster job, and a garage is no better. The only virtue of garage-cleaning is that there are no stairs to climb. You can charge by the day, the half-day, or the hour. If you cannot gauge the time needed to do the job, it's probably best to charge by the hour. If you should be asked to estimate for the whole job, give yourself plenty of leeway and give your customer a "not-to-exceed" dollar figure that compensates you for the worst that can happen. If you do the job in fewer hours, you can always take a bit less money. But remember—what you do is worth what you get!

Helping Senior Citizens

You can give a helping hand to older people free of charge or ask less for your services than you would for others. Your "profit" may be simply the pleasure of helping; it could also give you some career ideas and the benefit of older people's living and working experiences. If you find you like working with older people you might decide to go into social work, nursing, or some other field related to helping others.

Older people are increasing as a percentage of our population, and this is changing the way many of them live. Instead of living with their children, or keeping the homes where they raised their families, many older people move to retirement complexes and nursing facilities. Here, those who wish to live independently can do so among people of their own age. These retirement facilities may offer a variety of opportunities for you.

Begin your job efforts by putting up flyers on the bulletin boards of retirement homes (with the administrator's permission). The flyer could offer services from dog-walking to writing letters for the visually impaired. Other activities could include running errands, watering plants, and housecleaning.

If you have a driver's license, you can be doubly helpful.

Many older people have stopped driving but still have energy for visits and shopping. Some may still own a car in which you could take them where they need to go.

Not all older people are so energetic. If someone hires you to sit for an elderly, frail person, ask for a "help list" giving telephone numbers of relatives, the doctor, and emergency services. Also, ask about the person's interests and needs. Your pleasure in your job will be greater if you know what the person likes to talk about. Even though you may not know much about their experiences, you can be a good listener and will probably learn about things you would never have heard of otherwise.

Using Your Special Talents

If you are naturally gifted in some way, you can probably market your talents. If you excel in tennis, ballet, skiing, or playing the piano, you can be a tutor and give lessons to children—or adults. Adults who tutor in these areas make excellent earnings, usually by the hour, or with a fixed price for each lesson in a series. If you are very good at what you do, there is no reason why you should charge much less than adult rates.

You may be a whiz with a computer. Computer and word processing skills are something many adults don't have. In fact, some have an actual fear of computers. If you are computer-wise, you can probably find many adults willing to learn the basics. They may need to understand their home computer instruction manuals or how to operate a library's book-search computer.

Just as in other suggested work areas, you can market your talents best through word-of-mouth advertising and flyers posted in public places. For instance, if you are an excellent ice skater, you might post a notice at your skating club or rink offering lessons (or you could teach through the rink itself as an instructor). If tennis is your game, let local school athletic departments know you're available for lessons or coaching.

TEEN EMPLOYMENT AND EARNINGS

	Percentage of teens employed	Average weekly earnings
NATIONAL	65%	$35
Male	62	$43
Female	68	$27
Ages 13 to 15	63	$21
Ages 16 to 17	67	$54
White-collar background	68	$40
Blue-collar background	62	$29
East	63	$35
Midwest	72	$28
South	59	$43
West	65	$33
Central cities	61	$42
Suburbs	63	$29
Rural areas	68	$36

Source: Gallup Youth Survey, 1987.

Please comment on any jobs you've had, or work you have done for money. Tell me whether they've been enjoyable, and how they have helped you meet your money needs.

Lawn moving service (weeding, raking leaves also)—enjoyable because it is physical work that gives my body good exercise. *Baby-sitting*—a tough job because I'm too lenient on bedtimes. I don't baby-sit too often. *Painting*—even less frequently. This job gives me the satisfaction of knowing I did a good job. (It's easy, and I can do it in my own style.) *Snow shoveling*—a physical strain on my back, but it supports my financial demands during the winter months. Most of my work and earned money comes in the spring–summer–fall.

—Matthew Oberholzer

I never really had a job, but I've done things like cleaning up someplace for money. I feel that it's enjoyable if you think of the money that's going to be made.

—Melanie Bryant

I work in place of my brothers or with them. I think they keep me busy and meet my money needs.

—Christopher Oberholzer

CHAPTER 9

Finding a Job Out There

Teens of all ages are a large part of the work force just as they strongly influence the consumer market. About half of American teenagers thirteen to fifteen work part time, and they earn on the average $21 a week. Teens sixteen to nineteen work part time during the school year and full time in the summer. Teens sixteen and seventeen average $54 per week. Boys in both age groups earn more than girls because their jobs, whether at home or outside, are better paid.

How do parents feel about their children working? They generally have no problem with summer jobs. In the school year, it may be a different story. A family may vote a strong no if the adults feel that a job may interfere with grades, school activities, or simply a good night's sleep. If after-school work threatens your graduation plans, it's not worth it. You need at least a high school diploma to get a job with any promise of a future.

Some parents hesitate about jobs for another reason. They realize that teen goals are immediate, personal, and expensive. Young people want motorbikes, stereos, and designer clothing, for starters. Parents often think that these things are too luxurious (or in the case of motorbikes, too unsafe) for their children even if the kids spend their own earnings.

Many parents who limit their teens' money-earning do so from the very real fear that the money will be spent on alcohol and drugs. This is now such a real-life problem that even the most trustworthy teen may have to discuss it with his or her parents.

This can be done in two ways—and to clear the way for getting a job you may have to do both. One is to bring up the subject before your parents do by telling them exactly what you *do* plan to do with your earnings. The second is to keep accurate records of what you earn and where you spend it and offer to share these figures with your parents.

A job—even a part-time job—represents a big step toward independence in your life, and it's a big change for your parents, too. Things will go better for everyone if you are willing to demonstrate that you can handle the new responsibilities that having your own earnings will bring you.

But mostly, parents are pleased when their children earn money outside the home. They are glad for help with things that are simply outside the household budget. Your paycheck may also help with daily expenses or your future college tuition. Bringing up kids today is a very expensive business, and sending them to college can cost a king's ransom. So it's helpful to share the wealth.

When you spot a job opening, you should be prepared for an interview. Although some jobs may involve no more than a casual "You can start tomorrow," many places do interview prospective employees.

When applying for a position, ask for an application. Fill

out the form and arrange for an interview with the manager
of the business. If your application is put on file because
there are no openings, check back regularly to see where
you stand. Turnover may make your "on hold" status brief,
so keep checking, or someone else may get the job.

By the time you meet with the manager, he or she may
have checked out the references given on your application
and considered your experience, if any. Managers lean
toward those whose preference in working hours coin-
cides with the busy times of the business, so be as flexible
in this respect as you can.

Employers look for enthusiasm and interest as they
interview potential employees. As one fast-food manager
put it: "The person who is self-assured and pleasant during
my interview is going to reflect that confidence to
customers."

Before your interview, you might visit the store or restaurant at which you would like to work, to get a feel for the
place. Be discreet about this, but you might ask employees
or even customers what they think of the place and what
the management seems to look for. Even before you complete an application, you might visit and observe the
operation for yourself; often, you can get a sense of how a
place would be to work in just by observing the employees
and the customers.

When it comes to money, don't hesitate to ask for your
fair share. Although minimum wage is generally the starting policy, salary can sometimes be negotiable. If you have
handled money as a salesperson or have worked in a retail
store, you may be able to persuade the management that
you're worth 15¢ an hour over the minimum. If you are
experienced, ask if you will be able to move to the next
salary level before your scheduled salary review time.

Age makes a great difference in getting a job. Early teens

are, of course, going to find it tougher to enter the job market than their older brothers, sisters, and friends. But at sixteen you may find it hard to get the kind of job you want, and even eighteen-year-olds may find themselves unemployable in certain areas. It gets frustrating! You simply have to keep looking until you find the jobs that are available at your age level.

If you are fourteen or fifteen, the federal Fair Labor Act says you cannot do hazardous work such as running machinery or taking on second-story window-washing. In fact, even a cooking job is out because of the possibility of burning yourself.

Most jobs open for this age group are unskilled and involve activities such as food-stand sales. New Jersey's Great Adventure amusement park, for instance, hires fifteen-year-olds to sell pretzels and cotton candy. Even these jobs require working papers and a Social Security number. (If you are older and earning a substantial amount of money, you will need to pay into the Social Security system and probably pay a federal income tax. You can write to the Internal Revenue Service for a booklet that covers these details.)

What is available in job-hours for the teenager? You can seek out a year-round or a part-time job, a holiday position, a summer job, or a combination of all of these.

Over 27 million of you look for money-earning opportunities each summer. Check with youth agencies in your town, township, or county. Other job sources include county park departments, school counseling offices, summer camps, supermarket bulletin boards, and newspaper "help wanted" ads.

The Yellow Pages telephone book is also a good source of possible jobs. As an example, let's take animal care jobs. The Yellow Pages directory in one medium-sized city listed

24 animal hospitals, 14 pet shops, 14 kennels, 13 stables, 11 riding academies, 11 pet groomers, 6 trainers, 4 tropical fish dealers—and one pet cemetery. Surely, among all those places, there would be a job for you. The animal care field is full of teens giving a hand to professionals.

Other professional services in the Yellow Pages may offer job possibilities: carpenters, caterers, answering services, children's party-givers. People in these job areas often need a helping hand—maybe *your* hand.

Stores and restaurants, especially those in resort areas, need extra help in summer when Americans pack their vacation bags and take off. Many stores look for teens to help out or to replace vacationing employees. Other businesses that need extra summertime workers are lawn services, golf courses, and pool maintenance companies.

In a recent year, *Seventeen* magazine asked teenagers how to get summer jobs. "You can't be passive about job-hunting," said sixteen-year-old Stuart Niecko of Portage, Michigan. "You've got to get out and actively *search*."

Carla Owens, a high school senior of Atlanta, Georgia, suggested: "Begin your job search early. Spring vacation is not too soon to start combing your area for work." Craig Diamond, fifteen, of Malibu, California, said it's best to be persistent and aggressive. During a recent summer, Craig went door to door asking business establishments if they had work. Finally landing a job as a waiter, he was paid minimum wage plus tips. That may not sound impressive, but his total take for the summer was $3,000.

Most teens who capture part-time jobs "earn" their luck. First they spread the word that they're looking. When they are interviewed, they impress prospective employers by showing determination to get a job. If you're determined to make a summer job your goal, you will probably succeed. Goal-minded people are winners.

Let's say now that you have managed to land a summer job. How do you keep it? Arnie Runestad, in charge of employer-employee relations for over 300 Haagen-Dazs ice cream stores, said: "The biggest problem we have with teenage employees is responsibility—or lack of it." Runestad noted that teens often do not arrive on time or follow their schedules. On the other hand, Runestad pointed out, employers make mistakes, too. They often fail to tell their employees just what is expected of them.

Obviously, good communications are needed for a happy summer job experience. Here are ways to help keep the communication lines open:

- Be sure you understand exactly what your assignment involves.
- Tell your boss if you have any special problems, such as certain hours a week when you cannot work.
- If you see a potential problem, clear it up with your employer before it becomes an issue.
- Tell your boss if something is wrong with the way your job is going (you may find, for instance, that you are doing tasks that weren't part of your original work assignment).

A good working relationship with your boss can actually help you move ahead. He or she may be impressed with your work as, say, a waiter or waitress. Your good work may move you up the salary scale as you are promoted to dining room host or hostess. Or you may move up from junior to senior counselor if one of the summer camp staff has to be replaced.

A young Chicagoan, Maxine Bischoff, was prop girl for a summer-stock theater. She was so good at anticipating the items needed for approaching shows that the director recommended her to a New York producer. Now, at twenty-one, she is overseeing props at one of New York's major theaters.

While jobs do exist in interesting areas such as summer theater, the majority remain in the retail and restaurant businesses. The opportunities in fast foods outrank all other job areas. The question is, can you meet the challenge of life in the fast-food lane? The work pace is intense. Be prepared to use those six hands you never knew you had! While some young people enjoy the pace, others find the work tiring, boring, and demanding. Other restaurants with a more personal touch and an easier pace may be preferable.

In store work, everything is available from selling shoes to working as a stock clerk. Malls, of course, are prime sources of retail jobs. But don't wait until the last day of school to try and find work. Begin looking early in the year. That way, you may be able to start your job soon after school is over.

There are also volunteer summer and after-school jobs that may lead to financial opportunities later. Volunteer jobs range from assisting in hospitals to working at summer playgrounds. Jobs as library and museum volunteers often open up during the summer, too.

The highest plus in volunteering is that it gives you experience in a particular field. Experience is often *the* factor in getting a paying job later. How often have you heard someone say, "They won't give me a job because I don't have experience—but how can I get experience without a job?" Volunteering can often solve this problem.

Volunteering can also help you decide whether you like the field you're planning to work in. You may find hospital work depressing, or child-care a bore. By volunteering, you can test the waters without committing yourself.

You also feel good when you volunteer. There's a nice glow that comes from helping. Trevor Farrell, a resident of the Philadelphia area, certainly knows the feeling. Trevor made national news by helping homeless people. His campaign to feed and clothe street people brought him heavy media coverage. This in turn brought in money for his project. Trevor, now sixteen, has profited in several ways from this experience. He has found that social work is a field he may consider. He has worked extensively with adults, gaining skills he would not otherwise have at this point in his life. Most important, he has done something to make him proud of himself.

For the low-income or disadvantaged young person, summer jobs are very hard to find. The federal and state governments are trying to help minority youth—black and Hispanic youth, rural youth, and children of low-income families of all ethnic backgrounds—in finding jobs. Cities, towns, villages are also acting to help students find work. Even private industry is getting into the picture. State agencies are urging large companies to hire and train young people whose families have financial problems. This new approach is opening up thousands of jobs across the country each summer.

If you live in an area where you and your friends have little chance of finding a job, call your neighborhood or city business offices (found in town halls, borough offices, etc.). These places will be able to direct you to programs that help teens find jobs, or perhaps train them for jobs. These organizations have such titles as the Job Corps, the Neighborhood Youth Project, and the Training and Employment Program.

Also, ask your school counselor for help. Junior and senior high schools have become increasingly active in helping disadvantaged students find summer jobs. They realize that the sooner these students get experience in a field, the more likely they will be able to work in the summers to come.

The California Conservation Corps is the country's oldest community service program. Two thousand older teens sign up for a year-long stint of clearing streams, maintaining parks, restoring historic buildings, and fighting forest fires. The pay begins at $500 a month. At the end of the work-year, members are eligible for a $500 cash bonus or a $1,000 college scholarship. Students in Alaska, Connecticut, Minnesota, Ohio, Texas, Washington, and Wisconsin can find variations of this model California program.

The work opportunities offered by New York City's Volunteer Corps are also encouraging. Most of the projects are community-oriented, so students feel good about the work they are performing. Recently, older teens spruced up fifteen senior citizens' centers, supervised the distribution of new clothes to the homeless, and installed smoke detectors in low-rent apartments.

Many school districts encourage students to attend vocational school. Learning a trade is one of the best ways to get a foot in the job-market door. In Pennsylvania's Montgomery County the schools, the townships, and local businesses cooperate to put fourteen- and fifteen-year-olds in jobs. Students rotate through six shop areas, learning practical skills and receiving career information. They are then assigned summer jobs at minimum wage. Some go to area YMCAs, others to the Montgomery County Housing Authority and the U.S. Postal Service. When the summer is over they have worked hard and been paid for their efforts.

A small group of minority teenagers was given a great job opportunity in the summer of 1987. The field was one that most teenagers would pay to work in—the recording industry. Thirty-six teens were accepted under a program called YES, for Youth Employment Summer Jobs. They reported to the A&M Records headquarters in Los Angeles to sample the workings of the music industry firsthand. Their training consisted of practical advice, counseling, and skills training.

This unusual employment program grew from a volatile background. The National Association for the Advancement of Colored People (NAACP), the Black Music Association, and other black organizations had charged the recording industry with discrimination in hiring. Those who work behind the scenes in this field are virtually all white, and male.

The discrimination would be difficult enough if the industry profits came totally from record sales to white customers. But it is truly unsettling that the minorities are so underrepresented in a field where black recording artists and their fans are responsible for more than 25 percent of all the records and tapes sold.

When the teens had their first session at A&M Records, they were a bit uptight, but they soon loosened up as they rattled off their musical preferences. It turned out that their familiarity with A&M Records was largely due to Janet Jackson and her recent hits for that label.

A&M President Gil Friesen told his summer interns that they were really needed. "We have plenty of talent in singers and performers," he explained, "but there's a shortage of in-house workers."

The study released by the NAACP revealed that black and white music industries have separate management departments and that black personnel work almost exclusively with black music divisions. Blacks are only truly represented when they own a recording company, such as Motown or Stax.

Billboard magazine pointed out that in 1986 among the rock superstars were Michael Jackson, Lionel Ritchie, Prince, Janet Jackson, and Whitney Houston. The four largest-selling pop singles were by black artists.

Not all the A&M summer employees were from the Los Angeles area. Some came from Atlanta, Chicago, and New York. They were placed in radio stations, record stores, on magazine staffs, and in other areas. The training program prepared them for the various challenges they might meet, from answering a company's complicated phone system to directing people to the proper recording studios. For this backstage work, the pay was $200 a week.

Their participation, Friesen said, may signal the beginning of a steady flow of minority youth into an industry already profiting from black talent. Part of the YES teens' good experience came from giving the job their best effort.

All students who find work will have happier summer experiences if they give their employers cooperation and interest. There's a simple way to tell if you made a hit with your boss: If you're invited to work part time through the year or to come back next summer, you know you were an asset to the business, as well as accumulating assets of your own.

CHAPTER 10

Operating Your Own Business: Is It for You?

Most people think of "working" as being on the job in someone else's business from nine to five Monday through Friday, doing a job for which they have been trained. (The hours may vary, but the idea stays the same.)

Some young people think of "working" in very different terms. Their business hours may be far longer, and their "job" may be riskier than most. On the other hand, their rewards in money and satisfaction are often far greater than those enjoyed by the average job-holder.

These young people do more than work in business. They *are* their business, and their own boss.

Some of these businesses involve inventing, while others don't depend on new ideas to succeed. However, all have certain things in common. For one, their young operators are supplying items or services that people need or can be persuaded they need. For another, these businesspeople are determined to succeed, no matter what the odds or the obstacles. Once you've read some of their stories, you will be in a better position to decide how good an idea a business of your own would be. (It's not right for everyone.)

Not everyone who finds an automobile hubcap turns it into a business, but that's what Joseph and Manuel Nevera did. When they were eight and six years old, the Hazleton, West Virginia, brothers sold the hubcap at a nearby flea market for $5, with which they launched their business.

Today, not too many years later, the Nevera brothers have found, collected, swapped, bargained, bought and sold, to create a gigantic secondhand business. They have hubcaps—over 2,500 of them—hanging from rafters and overflowing bins and boxes. Ax handles, secondhand canvas covers, antique tools, old books and magazines—you name it, the brothers probably have it for sale.

As an offshoot, their American Historical Museum (admission, 50¢) features a Civil War cannonball, a complete and original 1880 stagecoach, early railroad lanterns, fur trapper's tools, even 300-million-year-old fossils the boys collected from a strip mine. Every item relates to local history.

Everything the Neveras buy, sell, and collect is done entirely on their own, without affecting their schoolwork. Their business, including the Museum, has entirely taken over a 200-foot-long building their father built—originally for his business!

At the other end of the business scale is Chris Urban of Vineland, New Jersey. Chris used his curiosity to create something brand-new. When his sneakers wore out, he didn't throw them away. Instead, he took them apart to learn how they were made. Finding a hollow area in the plastic framework for the sole, Chris "... began to wonder what to do with the space." His answer was to fit a flat battery and wiring into each opening and to add red safety lights to each side. He named his idea "Urbanites," and his shoes won a $3,000 prize offered by a battery company. Chris is pursuing his inventive streak at one of the most suitable colleges in the country—the Massachusetts Institute of Technology.

Although he's still in his teens, Dan Hallett of Los Osos, California, now grosses more than $100,000 a year by making crafts that combine ceramic seashells and driftwood pieces. He has enlisted family members to help run the business, which began with a $20 investment in supplies, driftwood that Dan picked up—and the idea of putting the two together.

Dan's products are now sold through more than 300 outlets around the country. Even with all the time the business takes, Dan plans to attend college and major in (what else?) business.

An entrepreneur who's too busy making money to go to college is Brandt Legg, of Fairfax, Virginia. At age nineteen he was worth more than $12 million as the owner of twenty-two corporations. Brandt claims to have built his empire by completing everything he has set out to do.

Brandt began by buying a first-day-issue stamp for 25¢ and selling it almost immediately for $85. Within four years he had built a stamp collection worth $100,000, and by seventeen he owned a stamp auction that brought in $1 million a year.

Stamps may appeal only to the collector, but food appeals to everyone. Here are the stories of three young people who have built highly successful businesses by capitalizing on this universal taste.

With a $5,000 loan and some design help from his father for his distinctive cone-shaped sales stand, Scott Paulson of Fort Worth, Texas, created a snow-cone business, Sno-To-Go, when he was fourteen. With two stands each netting him more than $1,000 a week, Scott was well on his way at last report. His plan was to take his company nationwide.

Kenneth Carter of Gary, Indiana, has been a cooking enthusiast since age five, but it was not until he attended a hotel banquet in New Orleans and saw how good food was prepared that he became seriously interested in catering. At twelve he turned interest into reality as first a volunteer and later a paid employee for a local caterer. Months later, and despite discouragement from friends he had hoped would help, he founded TC Catering Service at thirteen. With long hours and hard work, his business did succeed (his first job included last-second cutting up of 500 chicken wings when the supplier delivered them unprepared).

In its second year Kenneth's business grossed $10,000 and continued to grow, despite such problems as his being too young to withdraw money from his own bank account, and being turned down for a contract when he told his age (he never did again). Now, TC Catering is prospering, and Kenneth has received national media attention. He plans to attend either the famed Culinary Institute of America or Cornell University's School of Hotel Management when he graduates from high school.

When she was eleven, Kim Merritt of Cumberland, Maryland, began molding chocolate with three patterns her grandmother had bought her. Now, after years of hard work and a recent $75,000 business loan, Kim owns her own custom chocolate molding factory. Her motto is, "Never give up," and she puts in fifteen-hour workdays to gross some $250,000 a year. She credits support by her parents "all the way" for her success.

Other young people have created a wide range of businesses, from the solid to the silly. Here are a few samples:

- Joanne Marlowe started a mail-order crafts company at home when she was twelve and now heads her own women's clothing business that grosses over $2 million a year.
- Jason Hardman of Elsinore, Utah, founded a library when he was twelve because he grew tired of going six miles to a neighboring town for books.
- Cara Connery was thirteen when she requested and received recipes from celebrities for a cookbook that she published, with the profits going to the American Cancer Society.
- Agragone Eastwood DeMello was already enrolled in college at age ten. He was such a computer genius even then that he earned money by teaching computer science to adults.
- Two youngsters, Rawson Stovall of Abilene, Texas, and Amy Walterscheid, were ten and twelve respectively when they became practicing journalists. Rawson started "The Vid Kid," a computer column, and Amy became a reporter on young people's affairs for a TV station in St. Louis, Missouri.
- Three young people in Granite City, Illinois, started a summer camp for dolls, complete with tiny T-shirts, a camp photo, letters home, even a swimming certificate (without getting the dolls wet!), all for $29 per "camper" for a six-week season.

Now that you have seen what some young people have accomplished in businesses of their own, the next logical step is to see what goes into operating your own business.

"Logical" is indeed the operative word. It's better to be

coldly logical than highly emotional about your approach to starting a business, no matter how exciting your idea may be. Be logical about being sure that what you'd be doing in your business is something you wouldn't mind doing a lot of—because, if you're successful, you will be.

Ask your parents for suggestions, and perhaps for help. Some of the entrepreneurs mentioned got started with loans or other help from parents and other family members. You may be able to do the same. But if you borrow family money for your business, you may have to get your family to be flexible about repayment, since any money you make at first should probably go back into the business.

Be logical, too, about the time your business may take. Enough time should be available to let you do things right, which will probably be more time than you have estimated. Be sure to schedule business time so you can still keep up with schoolwork and your other responsibilities.

As you start, start slowly. If you plan to make a product, make samples to test the market, rather than cranking out a lot of gadgets you're not able to sell. You can use the samples to take orders, then make the products to fill them.

It will pay to do some long-term planning about the prices of your products or services and your business costs. If you plan to compete with operating businesses, can you do so and still make a profit? Can you forgo profit for a time to handle your start-up costs and get your business rolling? If so, for how long? These factors are not easy to judge; many an adult business doesn't make it because expectations (and expenses) are too high.

Yours will probably be the sort of business for which advertising (or, even better, free publicity) is a key to sales. Since people need to know what you have for sale and how to buy it, spending time and money on properly placed advertising is a must.

Can you go it alone, or should you have business partners? This is a very important question, with no one right answer. Partners share the expenses, the work, and the profits—in theory, at least. The reality often is that one or more of these sharings may not happen. Your partners may not have quite your degree of enthusiasm for the venture. Or the results may not be worth their involvement of time or effort. Of course, there are many exceptions, but as a very general rule partnership is not the best way for a small business to begin—especially if an enterprise largely reflects one person's ideas, ambitions, or both.

While it's true that operating a business isn't for everyone, it may be right for you. If it is, you'll find that nothing else will give you that extra measure of satisfaction that comes from being the boss.

CHAPTER 11

Planning for College: A Matter of Mind and Money

oday, 74 percent of Americans have completed high school, and more than half of all high school graduates go on to college. Higher education is becoming increasingly important to future success. As the world grows more service-oriented and jobs become more specialized, the college degree has become the starting point for nearly every well-paying career. Advanced degrees, too, are rapidly increasing in career importance.

A recent U.S. Census Bureau study showed that college graduates have almost twice the average monthly earnings of high school graduates, and holders of advanced degrees do even better.

- High school graduates earned $1,045 per month.

- Bachelor's degree graduates earned $1,910 per month.
- Holders of professional/advanced degrees earned $3,871 per month.

The essential role that a high school diploma can play in your future is shown in the same survey. Those without high school diplomas earned an average of only $693 a month.

Clearly, college is important to your entire future. The whole question of getting a college education is one you should begin to consider early. Your freshman year in high school isn't too soon to start planning. And your plans should include money ideas. You and your parents will need to plan carefully, and to take advantage of every financial break you can get. Unfortunately, college costs

EXPECTED SOURCE OF COLLEGE FUNDS

	From parents	Savings	Scholarship	Loans	Work
NATIONAL	57%	23%	22%	22%	17%
Male	54	27	22	24	16
Female	60	19	21	19	18
Ages 13 to 15	63	26	16	12	15
Ages 16 to 18	51	21	28	32	18
Above-average students	58	26	25	20	18
Average or below	55	19	17	25	15
White-collar background	59	23	22	26	15
Blue-collar background	58	23	22	17	22

Source: Gallup Youth Survey, 1987.

are growing far faster than the rate of inflation. By the year 2000, it is estimated that the cost of a four-year education in a private college may reach $100,000!

According to the Gallup Youth Survey, 57 percent of you expect your parents to pay a good part of your way through college, but you may have to help from a little to a lot, depending on your family's financial circumstances and your academic ambitions. Part of that help may be in re-paying your own student loan after you graduate and start to work. Your parents may agree to pay part of it for you, or to pay for a certain number of years before you shoulder the burden. Just don't forget that you or your parents or both will probably be deeply in debt after accepting four years of college loans. This could be a pivotal point in deciding whether you can afford college.

The answers to two questions will have a lot to do with the financial obligations you and your folks will have to assume regarding college:

1. What kind of college is right for you?
2. What sort of college career should you plan?

To answer question one, consider that there are many kinds of colleges with many financial structures, a number of which are relatively affordable.

Among the easiest to manage financially are two-year community or technological colleges. These offer associate degrees in a wide range of subjects. Community college technical degrees are designed to lead directly to skilled jobs in areas ranging from dental assistant to computer operator, from diesel mechanic to draftsperson. Associate degrees, usually in less technical areas, may allow you to transfer to a four-year college for the final two years leading to a bachelor's degree. (Transferring is made possible by the fact that many students drop out of four-year colleges in the first two years.)

Community colleges offer full- or part-time classes, often evenings as well as days, so it's possible to earn as you learn, perhaps with a part- or full-time job related to your field of study. Many employers work directly with community colleges to train prospective employees. Other companies hire employees, then train them at community colleges and pay part or all of the tuition.

Community colleges provide quality education without the expense of room and board. Four-year state colleges also keep costs as low as possible while providing the resources needed for a good education. State colleges often have branch campuses for live-at-home students as well as main campuses for resident undergraduates.

Private colleges tend to be the most costly of all—but service academies such as the U.S. Military Academy (West Point) and the U.S. Naval Academy (Annapolis) are the best college values of all: They're free to those who receive appointments. Of course, a graduate must agree to spend a specified time as an officer of the respective service. (ROTC in nonmilitary colleges can also offset academic expenses.)

By asking yourself the second question, what kind of college career you should plan, you approach the money question and others from a different perspective. For one thing, you are really asking whether you should go directly from high school to college or take time off in between. Also, should you attend college for four straight years without interruption? Your attitude and aptitudes will determine the answers.

For example, the high dropout rate among college freshmen and sophomores is because many high school graduates are not prepared to exercise the self-discipline demanded by college. For perhaps the first time in your life, you are completely on your own in all matters. As one counselor puts it: "Colleges...don't provide mothers to make you get up or turn off the TV...." Success or failure is strictly up to you.

If you're not the world's best time-manager, you may do better in college if you follow high school with a year or so of more structured activity. If you hold a job, others will count on you to arrive on time and to accomplish certain things once you're there. As long as your time-out isn't taken for some indefinite reason such as "getting my act together," it should work out to your emotional—and perhaps financial—advantage. Although military service takes more than a year, it can get you through college on the G.I. Bill, or you may even attend college or receive the equivalent in education and specialized training as part of your stay in the service.

A bit later you'll see how you may be able to pay a large part of your college education costs by extending the time you stay in college. Right now, however, one of the best ways you can be financially helpful has nothing directly to do with money. It's a matter of the grades you earn and the class standing you achieve, another good reason for planning your college career early. If you don't buckle down to getting good grades until your junior year you're already too late; your ninth- and tenth-grade performance is an important part of your college preparation.

You may score financial points later, then, if you can strike a good balance between grades, the scores you'll make on the standard achievement tests, and such extracurricular activities as band, sports, clubs, or student government. As a well-rounded person able to handle many things well all at once, you'll be in a better position to be accepted at one of the colleges you prefer.

Not everybody is an A student, but nearly everybody who wants to go to college can find a school where they can do good work, and get that much-needed degree. You'll be much happier in the long run if you can mesh your academic realities with your college goals.

Choosing the right college is as much an emotional as a logical decision. You may not altogether understand why, but as you search for colleges—especially as you visit their campuses—you'll probably recognize the one that's right for you. You may even get some positive "chemistry" from the catalog. As well as telling you the facts about a college, a catalog conveys something of the tone of the campus and may help you decide whether or not you'd fit in there.

Any college will be expensive, but there's encouraging news on the money front. Despite the cutbacks in government funding for student loans, loan money is still available. Family income alone isn't always the consideration it once was for acceptance or rejection of a loan application. Even if your family earns as much as $60,000 a year, some colleges will still offer some financial aid. It will be based as much on such expenses as having more than one family member in college at a time as it will on gross income. Not only that, but "found money" in the form of grants and scholarships can reduce the financial pinch for those who qualify.

The fully paid, four-year scholarship to an Ivy League college is almost as rare as the $1,000 Rolls Royce, but some $4 billion worth of help is available from more than 4,000 sources. These range from corporations and service organizations to ethnic associations and individuals. Qualifications usually include good grades, often in the top 10 percent of your class. (However, comedian David Letterman says—seriously!—that a C student can qualify for his scholarship to Ball University in Muncie, Indiana, his alma mater.) Otherwise, requirements may range from living in a certain state (the Boettchen Foundation Scholarships for Colorado residents) to demonstrating leadership qualities and financial need (Elks National Foundation Scholarships), or being a member of a particular ethnic group who meets certain academic requirements. Some scholarships impose limitations on what you may study, or require teaching certain subjects or in certain schools after graduation. Grants are usually outright gifts, awarded to those who meet specific qualifications.

You can find sources of scholarships and grants in several ways. Your high school guidance or vocational counselor may have lists of them. You can track them down yourself with some time spent in a library. Or you can use a computer search service ($39 to $259) to match your academic profile with scholarships and grants for which you might be eligible. The computer services use the same information you can find on your own, and there's no guarantee that a computer search will reveal every grant or scholarship for which you might qualify, but it is a time- and work-saver and may be worth the cost.

These grants and scholarships have strict deadlines for any academic year. Apply even a day late, and you're ineligible. Write for the forms you need early. Fill them out completely and accurately, and submit them on time. Apply only for those grants or scholarships for which you're eligible (each one spells this out quite clearly), but be sure to apply for all the ones you're entitled to. (One computer search firm estimated that $135 million in corporate, foundation, and individual aid went unclaimed in 1986.)

Another good piece of advice is to be persistent. Review scholarship and grant availabilities well before the deadlines for each academic year, not just when you're ready to start college. These awards may apply to ongoing students, so your freshman year college performance may earn you a sophomore scholarship or a grant that you did not receive the first year you applied.

Another source of funds is the work-study program. Many colleges offer such packages in which some of the earnings from a part-time job are applied to tuition or other college-related expenses. In such a program, course loads are adjusted to make part-time work mesh with classes.

The work-study program—or, for that matter, holding a part-time job on your own while attending college full time—may not be for everyone. When you're carrying a full academic load, that may be job enough. This is especially true during freshman year, during which more students flunk out or drop out than in the rest of college time put together. So unless you know from experience that you have the broad shoulders to balance both study and work, it may be wise not to take on both responsibilities right away. Also, by not rushing into work-study you can look around and see what part-time work is available; maybe you'll be lucky enough to find a job that ties in with your academics.

Another option worth considering is the co-op school. Some 175,000 students across the country are part of cooperative education programs. In these programs you alternative semesters, with one spent hitting the books, the next working at a job. Co-op courses exist for practically any field of study, but not at every college.

Co-op students learn to interrelate study and work. Just when classes get tiresome, you exchange them for a job, then reverse the procedure. Because they have demonstrated their job skills before graduation, co-op students tend to receive more and better job offers when they graduate.

Like work-study or a part-time job, co-op has its challenges. You have to keep your life in balance and accept the fact that co-op may add up to as much as an eight-year college career. However, it may enable you to afford a college that might otherwise be out of reach.

Now that you are aware of some of your college and money possibilities, how do you get the detailed information you need to make suitable choices?

First, talk to your high school guidance counselor to learn all the ropes of college selection and financial aid. Try to find books such as Peterson's *College and Cost Book* and *College Directory of Cooperative Education* by Stewart B. Collins, as well as the more readily available college guides and profiles. Write for college catalogs. Try to talk to people who have attended the colleges that appeal to you.

Then be on the alert for high school visits from the financial aid officers of colleges in your area, which usually take place in January. Even if an official isn't from a college you might attend, such a session can teach you a lot about putting the financial aid system to good use.

Finally, expect to work closely with the financial aid officers of the colleges that interest you. If your parents are applying for financial aid, they will have to make their recent federal income tax returns (and perhaps other financial information) available. You should be ready to do the same if you've earned enough to file tax returns on your own.

Because aid is probably available, you may not have to let a lack of money limit your college choice. If you're academically qualified for colleges such as Harvard, Yale, or Princeton—among other big-name institutions—go ahead and apply. Such schools are expensive, yes—but they may offer more financial aid to attract desirable students than less costly but less well-supported colleges.

No matter where you prefer to go for advanced education, from a major university to your local community college, you should apply for financial aid when you apply for acceptance, not later. By doing so, you'll be able to determine college costs fairly accurately before you make a decision. Only when you know what each college you like is going to cost and what aid might offset those expenses can you and your family work out the possibility of your being able to attend.

In computing college budgets, be sure to cover all your living expenses—dorm or off-campus quarters, dining hall, additional meals not included, laundry, phone calls, recreation, travel to and from home. Add these costs to tuition, room and board, books, lab fees, and such to arrive at your yearly total. Subtract anything that offsets this total, such as loans, grants, scholarships, gifts, work-study program earnings or credits, part of your co-op income, and other financial aid. Also, deduct any money you'll contribute directly from your savings or summer or part-time job earnings. What's left is the net cost of your college—and you and your parents will have to decide whether or not it's affordable.

One final thought about budgeting for college is managing your own budget. Even if your folks are paying your way, there will be certain expenses you alone should handle. As we said earlier the sooner you start budgeting your allowance and your earnings against your everyday expenses, the better prepared you'll be to do the same thing in college. One banker has said: "Too many college kids have no idea how to apportion their funds. They run out of money, borrow, run up bills, get into all sorts of trouble." If you get used to handling your money and your obligations now, your college money management will be a pleasant form of business as usual.

CHAPTER 12

What's On Your Money-Career Horizon?

We hope this book has sparked your thinking about how to earn, spend, and manage money. Many of the ideas you put to work for yourself now can continue to be useful in the career you select.

Your choice, of course, will be entirely up to you. But you might like to know what some teens think about careers and other things that lie ahead.

The Gallup Youth Survey of Princeton, New Jersey, regularly interviews more than 500 teenagers thirteen through seventeen about their opinions. In one recent survey dealing with career plans, three teens in four said they were planning on professional, technical, or managerial careers. Only 16 percent, or half the number of workers in the field now, said they expected to work in blue-collar occupations.

PROJECTED OCCUPATIONAL TRENDS

	1900 Census	1980 Census	2000?*
Professional and technical	4%	16%	64%
Managerial	6	11	10
Clerical	3	19	4
Sales	5	6	1
Blue-collar workers	36	32	16
Service workers	9	13	4
Agriculture	37	3	1
	100	100	100

* Percentages based on all teenagers naming a career choice.
Source: Gallup Youth Survey, 1987.

If these predictions about what teens will accomplish in the future are accurate, the work force in the year 2000 will have moved sharply away from today's emphasis on service industries, sales, and blue-collar jobs, reflected in the 1980 Census column.

The fields young people were choosing represent change, too. While young men continued a seven-year career preference for computers and electronics, business careers were regaining the popularity they had lost over the last twenty years. They had become the second choice for both young men and young women.

By showing strong preferences for medicine, business, and law rather than for secretarial work, the onetime first-place career, young women were reflecting great changes in job attitudes. Although traditional female careers such as teaching and nursing still ranked well, they were out-weighed by the new emphasis on male-dominated fields.

This was not true of women in computers and elec-tronics. Not long ago more young women were planning to enter this career. But with these anticipated changes in

CAREER CHOICES OF YOUNG MEN

1. Computers, electronics
2. Business
3. Skilled worker
4. Medicine
5. Engineering
6. Law
7. Military
8. Athlete
9. Fine Arts
10. Auto mechanic

CAREER CHOICES OF YOUNG WOMEN

1. Medicine
2. Business
3. Law
4. Secretary
5. Teaching
6. Beautician
7. Nursing
8. Social work
9. Sciences
10. Computers, electronics

Source: Gallup Youth Survey, 1987.

career preferences, many of the traditional male-female choices were no longer limited to one sex (nursing, however, failed to make headway as a male career, despite a severe shortage of nurses).

How do teens see their financial futures? Another Gallup Youth Survey reflected great optimism about earnings. One teenager in four expected to be making $50,000 or more a year by age thirty, while another 37 percent said they expected to be making from $25,000 to $49,999. Only 16 percent believed they would be earning less than $25,000 by age thirty.

The teens expected the present differences between what men and women earn for similar work to be erased in the future. They related scholastic achievement and learning ability very positively with career success. Nearly twice as many above-average students as average students believed they would be earning $50,000 a year by the time they were thirty. The occupational classes of teens' parents seemed to color their thinking about future earnings, too. Teenagers from white-collar families had higher expectations than those whose parents held blue-collar jobs.

Other Gallup Survey results may seem a bit odd when looked at alongside the optimism of tomorrow's salary expectations. Although seven in every ten teenagers stressed the importance of hard work to career success, this was a

QUALITIES CONSIDERED "VERY IMPORTANT"

	Respon-sibility	Honesty	Self-respect	Hard work
NATIONAL	89%	89%	87%	70%
Male	89	88	84	68
Female	89	91	90	71
Ages 13 to 15	89	89	85	69
Ages 16 to 17	89	90	90	70
East	91	88	88	65
Midwest	90	90	85	70
South	87	92	83	72
West	88	86	93	69
Central cities	95	84	90	78
Suburbs	86	90	83	69
Nonmetropolitan areas	88	91	88	66

Source: Gallup Youth Survey, 1986.

considerable drop from a 1984 survey, when the teens questioned gave hard work an 82 percent response. However, throughout the country and among teens of all ages, the traits of responsibility, honesty, and self-respect rated high in importance as ingredients of career success. Independence, patience, and obedience were also rated as important considerations by more than 60 percent of the teens surveyed.

Teen attitudes toward American corporations—the source of many young people's future careers—seem to be sympathetic. Today's teenagers apparently look with favor on the structure and operation of big business. Majorities in different age groups and with varied parental backgrounds believe that corporate profits are about what they should be and that federal regulation of corporations is at approximately the correct level.

OPINION OF CORPORATE PROFITS

	Too high	About right	Too low	No opinion
NATIONAL	29%	59%	6%	6%
Male	31	58	6	5
Female	28	59	7	6
Ages 13 to 15	29	57	7	7
Ages 16 to 17	30	61	5	4
White-collar background	31	60	4	5
Blue-collar background	27	57	9	7
Above-average students	32	58	4	6
Average and below	26	59	9	6

Source: Gallup Youth Survey, 1986.

FEDERAL REGULATION OF CORPORATIONS

	Should be more	Stay the same	Should be less	No Opinion
NATIONAL	14%	69%	12%	5%
Male	19	66	13	2
Female	9	72	11	8
Ages 13 to 15	13	70	11	6
Ages 16 to 17	16	69	12	3
White-collar background	13	70	12	5
Blue-collar background	15	68	12	5
Above-average students	17	66	12	5
Average and below	11	72	12	5

Source: Gallup Youth Survey, 1986.

Another interesting report from the Gallup Youth Survey says that some two thirds of all teenagers already have part-time jobs. When you add together the personal attitudes, job preferences, salary expectations, and favorable opinions of American business, one thing is clear: Most young people anticipate bright futures. They plan to make their way very successfully in occupations that are less defined by sexual conventions than they once were.

We wish you well as you prepare to take your place in tomorrow's interesting world. And we hope the money ideas presented in these pages will help you turn your talents and your ideas into shining reality.

THE BEGINNING!

Bibliography

Beery, Mary. *Young Teens and Money.* New York: McGraw-Hill Co., 1971.

Byers, Patricia. *The Kids' Money Book.* Cockeysville, Md.: Liberty Publishing Co., 1983.

Grenier, Mildred. *How Kids Can Earn Cash.* New York: Frederick Fell, 1970.

Hess, Karl. *Capitalism for Kids.* Wilmington, Del.: Enterprise Publishing, 1987.

Lee, Mary Price. *Money and Kids.* Philadelphia: Westminster Press, 1976.

McGough, Elizabeth, *Dollars and Sense.* New York: Wm. Morrow and Co., 1975.

Riehm, Sarah. *The Teenager Entrepreneur.* Chicago: Surrey Books, 1987.

Weinstein, Grace W. *Children and Money: A Guide for Parents.* New York: Charterhouse, 1975.

Index

A

advertising
  business, 113–114
  television, 24–25, 28
  teen services, 63, 65, 71, 75, 95
allowance, 1, 11–15, 17, 28
American Bankers Association, 43
American Express card, 49
attic, cleaning, 91–93
automatic teller machine (ATM), 48

B

baby-sitting, 63, 64
bank
  founding, 43–44, 55
  types of, 44
banking, 43–51, 55
bargains, shopping for, 34
Better Business Bureau, 40
bike
  all-terrain, 33
  buying, 35–36
  repairing, 74
bonds, buying, 56
boys
  and allowances, 11–12
  and baby-sitting, 62, 63

  and date costs, 19–20
budget, 6, 34, 36, 39
  college, 124
  designing, 16–23
business, owning your own, 108–114
Byers, Patricia, 69

C

California Conservation Corps, 105
car
  tips on buying, 36–38
  -washing service, 71–74
careers, teens' views of, 125–130
catering business, 111
cellars, cleaning, 91–93
certificate of deposit, 45
charge account, 39
charity, donations to, 6, 67
checking account, 44, 46–47
  misuse of, 48
chocolate-molding business, 111
chores, for allowance, 12
clothes
  budgeting for, 18
  buying, 34–35
college

planning for, 115–124
saving for, 6, 17
community college, 117
comparison shopping, 32–33, 38
complaint, with product, 39–40
Consumer Action Service, 41
Consumer Reports, 33
contract, for jobs, 62
cooperative education program, 122–123
cosmetics, shopping for, 36
Council on Family Health, 64–65
courses, baby-sitting, 64, 65
credit card, 47, 48–49
    age limit for, 39
    overuse of, 5

D
dating, costs of, 18–20
decisions, taking part in family, 8, 24
department store
    charge cards, 49, 50
    teenagers', 30
Diners Club card, 49
disc jockey service, 62, 69–71
discount store, 34, 35
dog-bathing service, 80–81
driver's license, 36, 93–94

E
effective annual yield, 45–46
expenses, budgeting, 17, 21
experience, buying, 8, 28

F
fair, running a, 67–68
financial aid, 120–121, 123

financial planning, 55
fish pond game, 67–87
friends, keeping up with, 26–27
Froese, Sandra, 60–61

G
garage sale, 62, 63, 68–69
gardening, 63, 88–89
girls
    and allowances, 11–12
    and baby-sitting, 62, 63
    and golf caddying, 78
    and lawn-mowing, 75
    sharing date expenses, 19–20
goal
    long-term, 21
    saving toward, 16
golf caddying, 63, 77–78
grants, 120–121
Grenier, Mildred, 82

H
handout, instead of allowance, 12–13
housepainting, 75, 89–91
How Kids Can Earn Cash, 82

I
independence, feeling of, 13, 26, 98
Institute for the Study of Finance, 55
insurance
    automobile, 20–21, 36
    industry, 55
interest, 54
    annual percentage rate (APR), 50
    compounding of, 45–46

rate of, 44, 45, 49, 56
saving cost of, 17, 39
interview, job, 98–99
investments, 58–59
*I Wish My Parents Understood
    Me*, 20

J
Job Corps, 104
jobs
    finding, 97–107
    summer, 55, 59, 67
    to supplement allowance,
        13, 16, 17, 28
    volunteer, 103–104

K
Kids' Money Book, The, 69

L
lawn-mowing, 62, 63, 75–77
layaway plan, 39
loan, student, 117, 120
love, money equated with, 4,
    6, 20

M
maid service, 66
mail order, 29, 35
MasterCard, 39, 49
material values, 5, 26
meeting, family, 7–8
mistakes, spending, 13
money, earning, 60–95
mutual fund, 57–58, 59

N
National Association for the
    Advancement of Colored
    People, 106

needs
    family, 9
    money, 1, 7, 13
Nonkin, Leslie Jane, 20
Neighborhood Youth Project,
    104
newspaper delivery, 62, 84

P
parents
    as cosigners, 48–49, 50
    doing jobs for, 61–62
    and money, 4–5
    working, 7
parties, children's, 85–88
partner, business, 114
party-helper, 66
passbook account, 44–45
payment, negotiating, for jobs,
    63, 69, 93
pet-sitting service, 80–81, 83–
    84
planning, 16
    business, 113
    children's party, 86
    for shopping trip, 32
private college, 118
prom, senior, 19, 27–28

R
recycling, 78–80
repair shop, 74–75
responsibility
    for auto insurance, 20–21
    of baby-sitter, 63
    parents', 9
    of teenage employees, 102
restaurants, jobs in, 103
retailers
    as job source, 103

and treatment of teens, 30–32

Riehm, Sara, 68

S

saving, 1, 13, 16
  toward auto insurance, 21
  toward large purchases, 32
savings account, 2, 6, 21, 38, 39, 43, 44, 45, 56
scholarships, 120–121
secondhand business, 109
self-reliance, learning, 6
skateboard, 36
spending
  by teens, 2, 6, 41
  increased, 5
  reasons for, 25–26
  tips on, 32
status symbol, money as, 2
stereo
  buying, 38
  for disc jockeying, 70
senior citizens, helping, 93–94
snow-cone business, 111
stamp business, 110

state college, 118
Stock Market Game, 53–55
stocks, buying, 54, 56–57
swap meet, 67–68

T

talents, marketing, 94–95
taxes, federal, 59
Teenage Entrepreneur, The, 68
thrift store, 35
tool, money as, 2, 4
Training and Employment
  Program, 104
treasure hunt, 87–88

V

Visa, 39, 49
vocational school, 105
Volunteer Corps, 105

W

warranty
  car, 37
  stereo, 38
work-study program, 122